THE WIZARDS BEHIND THE CURTAIN

How Blockbuster Trade Shows Got Their Start
from a Trade Show Manager Who Was There

RUSSELL FLAGG

Publisher's Information

EBookBakery Books

Author contact: flaggmgmt@msn.com

ISBN 978-1-953080-19-6

© 2021 by Russell Flagg

Cover design: Holley Flagg of
Flagg Design Graphics

Acknowledgments

A great thanks goes to Holley Flagg, my wife, graphic designer, artist, cheerleader, and supporter, who has contributed in every way to having me write this book. We have been married for as long as I have managed trade shows, over 50 years, yet there is a spark of love, hope, and discovery still with us. Yes, we are lucky people.

I would also like to thank Tracy Hart, for encouraging, extensive editorial input, and I. Michael Grossman, my amazing publisher for his rabbit-out-of-hat tricks. They made this book happen.

Finally, I want to pay tribute to all the trade show industry people who, like me, lived through Covid-19 without live events and their primary livelihood. It speaks volumes about the intrepid spirit that endures in our industry.

Table of Contents

January, 2020 - The Consumer Electronics Show (CES), was held in Las Vegas and hosted 4,000 exhibitors and attracted over 170,000 attendees. CES is the largest annual trade show in the United States.

1

A Look at Trade Shows
Call Me Ishmael

L ike the survivor and storyteller of Herman Melville's book, I may be one of the last survivors of an epic time in the 1970s when many major trade shows were started. This is a look at how some of today's events were developed back then. To borrow from John Bolton's 2020 tell-all book about the Trump administration, I was in 'the room where it happened.'

Numerous shows launched during the 1970s have become enormous economic enterprises. Charlie Snitow was a legendary producer of many of those trade shows, and he and his team started them over 50 years ago. They have continued into the 21st century as important marketplaces in a variety of industries. I worked on all of them.

The events listed below were live trade shows before Covid-19. They were active people-to-people enterprises in 2019 and for the first two months of 2020. After Covid-19, in March 2020, the entire trade show business ceased. From that time onward, exhibitions were postponed or re-scheduled as virtual on-line events. They still are the most prominent in their respective markets and will return as live events. Vaccinations and crowd immunity, as of June 2021, have opened the U.S. to everyday life. The pandemic and its death toll of over 600,000 lives must still be reckoned with in staging any live event.

The following are Charlie Snitow's trade shows still active today:

The National Hardware Show is the annual major show for hardware and home center retailers.

The Consumer Electronics Show is the largest annual trade show in America.

The SHOT Show is the largest military weapons and recreational shooting trade show in the world.

The Fancy Food & Confection Show - East in New York and West in San Francisco - are two major food purveyor trade shows in America.

The International Toy Fair completely fills the Javits Center for toy retailers and mass merchandisers each year.

The New York Automobile Show is the nation's leading event for Detroit and international car manufacturers and is the largest publicly attended event at the Javits Center with over one million show attendees annually.

The Accounting Show is an international event in 11 major financial centers in the United States, Australia, South Africa, Dubai, Canada, and Singapore. (I started the Accounting Show in New York, and it has become the premier event for the English-speaking accounting profession around the world.)

Charlie also produced a number of other major trade shows during that period, including: The National Furniture Show in Highpoint, North Carolina; The Eastern European Trade Fair in New York; and the Knitting Arts Show in Atlantic City in New Jersey (I organized and managed that event). These shows are no longer held. Their markets radically changed or moved offshore.

Although a relatively small office, Charlie and his team started and ran each show - closing sales, promoting attendance, organizing operations, with show-site management in a wide range of industries. I was active on all of them.

Developing new shows is like launching Broadway plays. The producer stands to lose his total investment and his credibility and reputation in the process. He is only as good as his last play. The trade show business operates the same way. The trade show producer must deliver solid business activity to be successful. It is the key to a show's continuity and its increased value as an ongoing business.

Both of my mentors, Saul Poliak and Charlie Snitow, were wizards in creating new events in robust and often untapped markets. Some markets did not even exist before their shows were launched. Charlie's SHOT Show is an example of an enormous firearms industry waiting to happen. Poliak and Snitow were accomplished in their craft. When they sold their businesses, a multi-million-dollar payday awaited each of them. The experience of working for these men was invaluable, and it set me on a path to start my own business.

Charlie liked to remind me, "Russ, when you start your own business, you can lose your money just like the rest of us. The secret is to work with people you trust and be lucky enough to find good markets."

Unlike Ishmael in New Bedford, my challenge was trade shows, not going to sea. It was important to establish my own ongoing business. Producing industry events, with money and reputation at stake, was a high wire act. It required attention to detail, analyzing the risks, gaining the support of the industry leaders, and then managing the event. Most of all, it required luck and timing.

A 19th century engraving of a sperm whale. The mythical giant was portrayed in Herman Melville (1819-1891) novel, *Moby Dick*, with Ishmael the lone survivor.

The bottom line: trade shows are a people-to-people business. Shows need people to be successful. At the same time, external factors, beyond anyone's control, can catastrophically impact on an event. Some of the stories in this book illustrate that truth; our business is always at the mercy of the unexpected.

In November of 2019, without warning, Covid-19 developed a world-wide epidemic. Within 90 days of being identified in Wuhan, China, it changed the world and its almost 8 billion inhabitants. It totally decimated the entire exposition industry across the globe.

Over 27,000 events world-wide were postponed, canceled, or repositioned as virtual events. Losses in the trade show industry were in the billions of dollars. All ancillary trade show activities and related labor-trades services ceased. Tens of thousands of trade show workers were furloughed or eliminated.

No one could have anticipated a worldwide pandemic eliminating person-to-person contact and live events. Remarkably, trade show DNA is still thriving in enterprising show producers. During the 2020 and 2021 epidemic, intrepid event managers met the challenge of Covid-19 with new and successful virtual events. They recreated existing trade shows as on-line Zoom meetings and markets.

The Consumer Electronics Show, for instance, the largest annual show in the United States in 2020, and the premier event Charlie Snitow and Jack Wayman launched in 1968, became a virtual event in January 2021. Major world-class events became virtual in 2021 to serve their markets, their vendors, and their buyers.

Like Melville's *Moby Dick*, our analogous great white whale, trade shows are alive in meeting the challenges of the Covid-19 epidemic.

The Crystal Palace, London, 1851
Prince Albert's extraordinary glass and cast-iron exhibition pavilion

2

The Trade Show Business
When Did It All Begin?

I suggest 1851. The Great Exhibition in London was inaugurated that year and was the first exposition created on a grand scale for the global market.

Europe was recovering from the Napoleonic War, as well as earlier wars and revolutions on the Continent. Concurrently, Great Britain established shipping prowess, with a mighty navy and a commercial fleet of clipper ships circumnavigating the globe. Prince Albert, Queen Victoria's consort, conceived this British commercial and cultural undertaking to promote trade with countries newly accessible. Key to his success was the partnerships he formed with British commerce officials and private business associates.

The German-born prince, an inspired leader, was the wizard and project manager of the event, with a startlingly new cast-iron and glass exhibit hall in Hyde Park. It enclosed 14,000 exhibits and 100,000 objects in a greenhouse on steroids. The glass halls covered 100 acres of country pavilions and provided natural light and open space unlike any building ever assembled. The show had miles of aisle carpeting, the latest Victorian décor, and thousands of live trees.

Stunning pavilions from over 100 countries at Hyde Park brought the rarest of cultural and fine art treasures, innovative machine-made goods, native handcrafts, and the latest Industrial Revolution inventions from every major country, including the electric telegraph and the steam engine. Six million visitors attended and previewed a new world's fair, with Indian crown jewels, the largest diamond in the world, Chinese silks, and exotic African woods.

It was a remarkable British achievement. Prince Albert instantly became a popular British Royal, and his Grand Exhibition was the model for world fairs for the next 150 years. He helped launch the Victorian Age, celebrating the Queen's vast colonial empire spanning India, Australia, New Zealand, Africa, Canada, and the Americas.

The Crystal Palace in New York followed in 1853 and replicated the innovative cast iron-and-glass London structure. It was erected on Fifth Avenue and West 42nd Street, where the New York Public Library now stands. This American Great Exhibition had marvelous national pavilions from four continents with priceless treasures from major countries and colonies around the world. The newest industrial technology, the latest manufactured merchandise, the most elegant cultural and fine arts, and international dignitaries in their native dress, all delighted the millions of New Yorkers and Americans who attended.

The trade show business today has evolved from these grand beginnings. They provide segmented and focused marketplaces supporting specific industries. Every sub-sector of the economy is represented by at least one trade show. Of the 27,000 trade shows worldwide, 35% are in the United States.

We exist in a world of instant information. Global events, stock markets, and everyday life are instantaneous. Google is our encyclopedia. CNN, *The New York Times, The Wall Street Journal*, and media outlets fill in the blanks. The Internet and cell phones are constant companions.

Trade shows have Crystal Palace DNA at work. Sellers need buyers. Buyers need sellers. Shows are the meeting places to conduct business. New trade shows are a way of life. Comic Cons have been created for comic book cosplayers and Hollywood producers. Sneaker Expo for collectors and the z generation. TED events for educational, cultural, and life-enhancement seekers.

The innovative steam engine of the Great Exhibition in 1851 is analogous to the dynamics of trade shows. When steam engines reach optimum speed, they operate on their own momentum. Brand-new shows in novel markets operate the same way. Momentum is achieved by the invisible hand of the industries they serve. Trade shows are the engines of commerce that have roared down the tracks from the 19th century into today's 21st century economy. It is my hope they will continue that journey.

Russell Flagg welcomes 1,500 CPAs at the annual California Accounting Show and Conference in Los Angeles, CA. Major trade shows serve multi-billion-dollar industries in every principal economic sector.

3

A Brief History
of a Trade Show Manager
and His Mentor

In 1969, Viet Nam was raging, antiwar activists were on the streets and on the campuses, Civil Rights movements were on the march. Meanwhile, some of us were getting jobs and supporting families.

With abilities that included attention to detail, organizing complex tasks, and a love of working with people, I found trade shows as a second career. My first career was with Alcoa in Pittsburgh and then Remington International in Bridgeport, Connecticut. Those two giant firms provided a requisite of corporate experiences: marketing aluminum products to American industries, then selling electronic products to international import dealers in Europe and the Middle East.

Working for huge organizations, however, had limitations. I wanted a smaller company where I could shine. That search led me to Clapp & Poliak, a major innovator in the emerging field of trade show management.

I was lucky to find Saul Poliak who recognized my talents and put them to work. Saul was my first mentor, and I worked on all of his industrial shows. Saul was a brilliant show producer, but after several years it was time to put that experience to work and start my own company.

My new firm was off to a good start and had launched two new shows, but it wasn't long before I would meet the P. T. Barnum of the trade show business – Charlie Snitow, complete with fancy vests and an ever-present large, Cuban-leaf cigar. His zest for life was palatable. A visionary and purposeful leader, Charlie was always on the lookout for new trade show business. The Consumer Electronics Show was started in his office in 1967 and grew to become the largest annual trade show in the United States.

In October of 1973, I first met Charlie in his office, where we discussed my new trade shows. I had suggested we might work together on them. Charlie expressed interest in both. One was Video Expo at the Plaza Hotel. The other was Travel Expo at Madison Square Garden. But five months went by and nothing came of it.

Then I got a phone call in March, 1974.

"Russell? Charlie Snitow here. I have some bad news. Bob Pomeranz (his longtime partner and brother-in-law), just had a heart attack. He's not expected to recover."

"Oh Charlie, that's terrible," I said.

"Certainly is. Was thinking back to our conversation a few months ago and wondered if you would be interested in coming on board. We need another experienced hand in the office. Can you come down to discuss this?"

"You bet."

We picked a time and met in his office. When I got there, I felt comfortable immediately. He greeted me like a long-lost cousin.

"I know it's early," he said, "but let's have a drink. Do you like vodka?"

We drank and chatted and agreed I could continue with both of my shows while working for him full-time. Just like Rick at the end of *Casablanca*, I might have said, "I think this is the beginning of a beautiful friendship." The only snag was that Charlie's organization had been acquired by Cahners Publishing Company, headquartered in Boston; I'd have to be approved by them.

I flew to Boston the next day and met with Saul Goldweitz, Cahners' president. After a cordial greeting and a review of my experience, Saul came right to the point.

"Why do you want to work for Charlie when you already have your own business?"

My answer was honest and direct. "I can learn a lot from him."

After a short discussion and a phone call to Charlie, Saul said I had the job as vice president working for Charlie Snitow.

It was a small office, with 15 managers and staff in total. From the first day in the office, he was the boss. A plain-spoken man, Charlie led with humor and a command of his enterprise. His sunny disposition overlooked the gaffes of his small staff. His focus was always on the business at hand. He said it simply: "Put your energy in the business, and everything else will take care of itself."

The Snitow organization owned every show it produced, with the exception of the Consumer Electronics Show. It was my job to work on all of them: The National Hardware Show, The New York Auto Show, the Fancy Food Show, and CES among others. All were cutting edge events in the industries they represented. They made a lot of money for Charlie.

Shortly after I started, Bob Pomeranz recovered from his heart attack and returned to the office. I was fortunate to stay on and continued to work with Charlie who became my mentor. He was a robust 65 years old, but as fit as I, 30 years younger.

He liked me and sought me out for what became a ritual 5 o'clock drink. I may have been a foil for his comradery and largesse, but I always looked forward to our conversation and libation. With his Cuban cigar and glass of vodka, Charlie was happy to share the day's news. He enjoyed holding court in his large, cluttered office. We became fast friends, with a boss and employee relationship during the day, then a more personal bond after 5 pm. Our conversations were far-reaching - music ('On the Road to Mandalay,' was a song from his school days he happily sang), art (he loved African sculpture), religion (he had a deep knowledge of the Torah, though he was not religious in a temple-going way), trade shows (he was proud of his accomplishments with the Consumer Electronics Show), and alcohol (Wyborowa Polish vodka - his brand of choice).

Relaxing with vodka after a strenuous day may have been inherited from his Russian immigrant parents. Yet alcohol never seemed to dull Charlie's legal mind. He'd graduated from Cornell University and Cornell Law School in 1930, co-founding the Curia Law Society after being told the existing legal clubs did not admit Jews. Perhaps practicing law during The Depression with his brother in-law developed his intrepid personality. Charlie was born in Hell's Kitchen in Manhattan, February 7, 1907, but he ended up owning homes in Scarsdale and Garrison in

New York and Grenada in the Caribbean - a departure from when his family lived above his father's small variety store on 10th Avenue and W. 59th Street.

Like the lawyer that he was, in conversations, he liked to ask for an opinion and listen for an answer. He enjoyed verbal ping pong, although sometimes he would defer from the game: "How should I know?" Charlie would say with a smile. "I only run shows, pay the bills, and keep everybody happy."

Building a loyal band of cohorts was Charlie's forte. He knew the value of his team in running his business, and his office staff was part of his extended family. If you were one of his managers, he would make sure you were included. "Where's Betty?" Charlie would say, referring to Betty Djerf, one of his key marketing managers. "Get her in here. She should know what's going on." Betty knew she belonged and so did every office member.

Once, I asked him, "Charlie, where did you find new ideas for your shows?"

"We were hungry for information," Charlie reminisced. "We got to know trade magazine editors and publishers. Those guys always had their antennae out for new ad revenue. We, in turn, were looking for new exhibit revenue. It was a good Mutt and Jeff relationship. We got to know who was buying and who was selling."

Another time I asked about funding new start-up shows.

"It's easy to lose money on a show," Charlie said. "The trick is to have the exhibitors invest their money from the beginning. They have to buy into the whole trade show idea. Their customers must equally believe they're attending a worthwhile event. Our job is to convince them both they are doing the right thing.

"We promise an event will happen at a certain time and place," he continued. "We have to deliver. Our reputation is at stake."

Charlie combined an old-world work ethic with an upbeat bonhomme. Knowing how to schmooze and when to flatter came easy to him. «Just part of the game,» he said.

Those abilities served him in meetings and lunches with top executives and industry leaders. He was a keen observer of people's foibles, but

14

seldom commented on them. "If we had to worry every time someone's feathers were ruffled, we never would have a business." His uncomplicated style of speaking could become more eloquent when speaking about subjects important to him. (Charlie sang in the Metropolitan Opera Chorus and said that singing under Arturo Toscanini was one of the highlights of his life.)

Charlie's most ambitious show was the World Trade Fair launched during the Eisenhower Administration in 1957. At the height of the Cold War and the Iron Curtain, Charlie attracted Communist-run Poland and Yugoslavia to his event, as well as 59 other nations from around the world. The Coliseum at Columbus Circle was the site of the two-week show in April, 1957, that attracted over 700,000 visitors with more than $1 billion in trade.

This was followed up with a perfect example of the force of his personality: in 1959, he convinced the Soviet Union, for the first time, to participate with an extensive exhibit of Russian products and technology. Charlie believed that his World Trade Fair, and international trade in general, could bolster the prospects for world peace.

During the Fair, he'd meet with Polish trade officials in his office with glasses of Slivovitz, a 100-proof plum brandy, to toast a new day at the show. He loved talking about those days.

"You could never keep up with those guys," he said. "Slivovitz was mother's milk for them, and they could drink it by the hour. Poland, Yugoslavia, and Russia, sent some of their best people to the United States for the World Trade Fair. Some were probably spies, for all we knew, but they were engaging and put a smiling face to the Cold War.

"We had a United Nations at the Coliseum with Communist officials, U.S. State Department officials, the FBI, New York City police, the media and the press, and 59 international exhibitors all in one place looking over each other's shoulders," Charlie said with a chuckle, puffing on his Cuban.

"President Eisenhower came to the show in 1959 when the Russians were there. And that was when the American U2 spy plane was shot down and Premier Khrushchev castigated Eisenhower for lying about aerial spying. Trade shows are meeting places for people, and we sure had them that year."

Charlie's independently produced shows bridged the gap between traditional trade association-sponsored events of the 1960s and 1970s, and the high-tech mega shows run by entrepreneurs today. Risk-taking, sales ability, and drive, were his unique talents to launch new events for the American economy. This was his story.

"My trade shows were the result of good timing and a lot of luck," Charlie said. "I've always been lucky I guess, with good friends and partners, and a business I really loved. Where else can you have Slivovitz at 8 o'clock in the morning with friends from Warsaw?

"The traveling salesman was replaced by retailers coming to meet their suppliers at our shows. It was a more efficient way to do business.

"Show business today is entrepreneurial. Our original trade shows were an entree to dot.com events that are like Star Wars movies today.

"It's a wonderful business we're in," Charlie said. "Trade shows are a way of life. We're lucky to be a part of it."

Charlie's uncanny ability to create new shows for new markets remains the touchstone of our business. A business I was proud to call a satisfying second career.

(This information was taken, in part, from the *New York Times* obituary of July 5, 2000, after Charlie's death on June 28, 2000, at the age of 93.)

CES is not only a trade show, it is an incubator for innovation and change. New players emerge with each CES event.

4

How CES Got Started
(Formerly, The Consumer Electronics Show)

The largest annual trade show in the world was created by a showman and a lawyer, both of humble beginnings. Jack Wayman, the showman, was the Executive Director of the Electronic Industries Association's Consumer Electronics Group (now known as the Consumer Technology Association). He started business life in Washington, D.C., selling TVs. Charlie Snitow was the lawyer and had become a major trade show producer. He started life in Hell's Kitchen.

In 1966, Jack was looking for an experienced trade show firm to help him launch a new show for consumer electronics. Giant electronics firms were spending millions on nationwide television, flogging TVs, tape decks, boom boxes, and every kind of home entertainment system. Jack's market was expanding: consumer electronics were hot. His CEA members were actively inventing and manufacturing the next wave of products every six months. The products were being sold through every retail outlet. Yet, the business event they were using, the National Association of Music Merchants (NAMM) Show relegated them to a corner of the show and Jack wanted more.

Jack wanted a dealer show where appliance chains, big box stores, discount outlets, drug stores, and hardware stores, could buy his members' consumer electronics. Dealers needed a warehousing show to stock their shelves for the next selling season. The CES moment had arrived. To generate new business for his members and income for his association, a trade show was the answer.

Jack's survey of New York trade show firms was almost complete. Charlie's firm was last on the list. Charlie's stage-like office was the setting for their 2 pm meeting. Jack planned a one-hour perfunctory visit, a simple hello and goodbye. He had tickets on the 5 pm Eastern shuttle back to Washington. At 5:30 they were still talking.

Charlie went into detail about how his dealer shows worked. The National Hardware Show was similar to what Jack needed: a warehousing event where dealers met manufacturers. It eliminated the local route salesman. At one place, at one time, hardware store buyers could see a plethora of sellers.

Charlie's company was ready-made for Jack's show. CES could be managed just like the National Hardware Show. Charlie's team was already in place: operations people, salespeople, back-office people. No other trade show firm had that set-up. Jack could run his new CES without an expensive start up. Just plug-and-play Charlie's show staff for *his* show.

After Cuban cigars, Champagne and vodka, and old-fashioned camaraderie, Charlie and Jack agreed to co-create a new event focused on consumer electronics. Jack would sponsor. Charlie would manage. The first show was scheduled for New York City in 1967.

The collaboration of these two showmen was the catalyst that sparked CES's initial success. Their DNA was the chemistry in the longevity and relevance of today's CES. Charlie was a P.T. Barnum producer and a charming and talented pitchman. Jack was a Barnum & Bailey showman, with theatrical presence and a commanding baritone voice. He was courtly, funny, and smart. He had a shock of white hair, the lively gait of a tennis player, and a rapid-fire repartee. Together they were a great match.

"None of us dreamed the show would take off as it did," Charlie said. "But there was keen competition among the American, Japanese, Korean, and European manufacturers. There was new demand for home electronics. That's wonderful chemistry to jumpstart a show.

"American consumers were already buying home entertainment. The show simply sped those systems to market. Jack's Board of Directors was primed for the show, and CES was lightning in the bottle. We had hardware show experience. They had the market. It was the perfect model, and Jack trusted us with his new baby.

"The 1967 CES show was a tremendous success. Retailers came from all over the United States, Canada, Latin America, Europe, and Asia.

"We were the stage managers for Jack Wayman. We focused the spotlight on him, gave him the script, and provided the applause track. It was a great symbiotic relationship that lasted 10 years. Eventually, CES ran the event on their own.

"Nothing lasts forever, and new association shows like the CES always have the potential to be taken in-house." Charlie took a puff on his cigar and offered a simple homily. "That's the way the cookie crumbles.

"We launched CES, and it was successful beyond our wildest dreams. We will never regret the good times and good friends we met during our time with the show. And Jack Wayman was one of the best damn showmen we ever met."

In January of 2020, the CES was held in Las Vegas, and hosted over 4,000 exhibitors and attracted over 170,000 attendees. Top CEOs from global companies were featured speakers. Over 5,000 journalists covered CES with tens of thousands of TV, radio, newspapers, on-line and business journals, reporting. Self-driving cars, electronic wearable fashions, digital health products and robots, exemplified the wide range of state-of-the-art products previewed. CES has taken on a life of its own. In 2021 it was purely digital and some 2,000 companies participated, and even more stories were written as journalists around the world were able to cover it equally with American journalists. The 2022 event is expected to be a hybrid - both physical and digital - with the best of digital global expansion combined with the five-sense experience and serendipity of a live, face-to-face exhibition.

CES is a trade show. It is also an incubator of innovation and change with new players emerging with each new Las Vegas event. Jack and Charlie started it.

* CES is a trademark owned by the Consumer Technology Association

The Grand Central Station clock
Charlie Snitow had a 5 o'clock ritual with Russ Flagg to discuss the day's
business and gossip.

5

Do You Know What Time It Is?

The office building at 331 Madison Avenue was the location where most of the Mad Ave agencies were headquartered in the 1970s. Brooks Brothers was two blocks north. Worth and Worth's hat store was on the corner. Arnold's deli was next to the entrance. The 1920's building elevators were original, with sliding glass-door conveyances operated by Max and Billy, two union guys. Joan, the receptionist would greet you when you arrived at Charlie's 10th floor, elegant base of operations. Like a ship's captain, Charlie would survey his office in the morning, greeting his crew. He had a fast-stepping gait, a kind of swagger like many self-made men, but his seemed quite natural.

Charlie was unique in the trade show business, launching events in over 10 new industries which established him as a major show producer.

Quips and banter were part of the morning ritual and were light-hearted and direct. "What's up with you today, Russell? You look sharp with your red tie."

He was a natty dresser himself in the ad agency style of the times. But under his fancy vest and British tweed sports coats, he was all business. His workplace was only 10 blocks from where he grew up, and he liked to remind us of his modest beginnings: "I've come a long way from Hell's Kitchen, and it is my fervent desire not to go back."

Charlie was easy-going and good company, but his determination was always in evidence. When not on the phone himself, he often walked down the corridors, listening in on us show managers, as we made calls on the latest phone systems. He'd offer friendly kibitzes. "When are you going to close the sale, bubbeleh? Get back on the phone and tell them you'll personally guarantee the show yourself!" he might say with a chuckle.

Relationships were forged and business conducted without ever meeting a person. Some managers used telephone headsets. You could see them gesturing in their office as they spoke. One manager had a mirror in his office to help with his body language. Show managers might make 30 or 40 calls on a typical day for one closing.

"Sales calls are like Broadway auditions," Charlie offered, one late afternoon with a glass in hand. "There's no guarantee you'll get the part, but you give it everything you've got. Rejection is part of our business."

Assisting us were our secretaries, pounding away at IBM Selectric typewriters outside of our cubicles. Everything was typed: letters, contracts, sales and payment records, invoices, advertising copy, and presentations.

The whole enterprise was a hive to close the sale, and Charlie's commitment to always do better kept it buzzing. He liked having smart people in his company, appreciated our efforts, but also knew how to unwind. I looked forward to when Charlie would stand in my doorway and ask, "Do you know what time it is?"

I did. It was time for our 5 o'clock afternoon ritual: Charlie's invitation to join him in his office for a drink. He did not want to drink alone, and I became his drinking companion.

Always the genial host, whoever was in his office as a guest, would probably be invited to partake. "Have a drink. Tell you what. Let's have one together. I'll show you a new drink I just invented. It's called a VoChamp. Vodka and Champagne. And it's guaranteed not to give you a headache. Vodka from Poland. Champagne from France. What could be better?"

His office was like a stage set. A British barrister's chamber. With Charlie's sharp wit and legal training, he could have played Charles Laughton in *A Witness for the Prosecution*. He'd sit regally at his desk in a large leather chair with an over-sized ashtray at one side. A long conference table with ten chairs stood in the middle of the 40-foot room, an elaborate chandelier hung above it. A bar with a mirror was at the far end, with a small refrigerator and ice maker underneath. Plaques, awards, and Cornell College and Law School diplomas, hung on wood-paneled walls close to his desk.

As Charlie's regular guest, my job was to set up the drinks: two Polish Wyborowa vodkas on ice in large tumbler glasses. It was his office and his bar, and I was the employee, but after 5 pm, it was two friends having a drink and sharing the day's activities. What was the latest gossip?

Charlie was a lawyer at heart, and with a drink and cigar, he would open with his thoughts of the day. He saved some of his best discussions for our afternoon drink, as he might if preparing a case or testing an argument. Some of my most informed insights into our trade show business originated in those afternoon sessions. Charlie was a good friend and a great mentor.

As we chatted and drank, Charlie's brother-in-law, Bob Pomeranz, was busy in his adjacent office. Bob chose not to drink in the office. He signed checks, paid bills, executed leases, argued with vendors, hired and fired. Charlie was the "good" guy; Bob was the "bad." He, too, was a very bright lawyer, but he went to great lengths to hide his intellect. Bob once said, "When Charlie was playing the lead in our school play, I was in the balcony focusing the spotlight."

Charlie balanced work with a delightful sense of play. He loved wine, women, and song. He enjoyed his privileges, had nice homes, collected art, and his Jewish faith was his bedrock. To be admired was his ability to project calmness in the most stressful of times. Charlie liked to say he had a soporific effect on anxious people higher strung than he. His sense of humor would emerge at the most unexpected times.

Once, there was a contentious meeting in his office with the National Hardware Association. They had come to New York specifically to see Charlie to demand a greater share of the National Hardware Show profits. In the middle of a heated discussion, Joan, his assistant, came in.

"Mr. Glazer is waiting outside to see you, Mr. Snitow."

"Well, send him in," Charlie said.

Mr. Glazer, formally dressed in a three-piece suit, looked like a proper burger from Germany, where he had immigrated from after the war. He presented himself with his suitcase, and with a great flourish, greeted Charlie with his hand at his chest.

"Guten Tag. I have something for you and your Gaten."

"Let's see it," Charlie invited.

Mr. Glazer plopped his suitcase on the conference table in the middle of show reports and briefcases. He opened it to reveal neckties of all designs; elegant women's scarves peeked out of one side.

"Italian silk ties. Women's silk scarves," he announced.

"How much are the ties?" one hardware executive asked.

"Five dollars, three for $10," Mr. Glazer said. "The ladies' scarves are $10 and the finest Italian silk."

Charlie's office was transformed from an arena of clashing titans to an impromptu haberdashery of excited shoppers. Executives held ties to their collars and discussed stripes versus prints. Some reached for their wallets, asking for change. Mr. Glazer had manila envelopes with metal clips for the purchases. One man bought a scarf for his wife. Almost everyone bought ties. The whole event lasted 20 minutes.

Charlie presided over it with quips and light humor. The meeting's contentiousness evaporated due to Charlie's spontaneity and Mr. Glazer's satisfying, silken inventory.

One afternoon, when I joined Charlie in his office, I noticed some African sculpture on his desk – objects of dark wood with large, round faces. They were about six inches high and looked quite old.

"Where did you get them?" I asked.

"They're Ashanti, from Ghana, and the round-faced ones are fertility symbols," Charlie said. "They're from my World Trade Fair at the Coliseum in 1958. We had 59 exhibitors from all over the world, and one was Ghana.

"They had a marvelous exhibit of exotic wood. Ghana was selling ebony and other rare woods, as well as coffee, some of the best in the world. They had tribal sculptures in their booth from their Ashanti people to show their native culture. They were kind enough to give me three. I have always had a warm spot in my heart for Ghana ever since. You never know when you might need a fertility symbol," Charlie said, chuckling.

"You know, the Coliseum was a helluva place to do a show. It had four floors and a parking garage, and the unions seemed to run the place. Exhibitors simply could not understand why they needed so much union help. The director from Ghana thought it bizarre that a union man unloaded their truck on the first floor, another ran the elevator to the second floor, and a third delivered their stuff to the booth.

"It's a wonder the Ghanaians found their way around the Coliseum with all the union help," Charlie said. "I look at those sculptures and think of the marvelous friends I met at the World Trade Fair.

"Now, Russ, set up our drinks. You know what time it is."

The 73rd Annual National Hardware Show at the Las Vegas Convention Center

6

The National Hardware Show

In 1946, Charlie Snitow was practicing law. He was a quick study and always resourceful in providing his clients with good business advice. That's why some of his hardware manufacturing clients sought his assistance in an entirely different arena.

They wanted to expand the number of hardware store owners and managers they dealt with and thought a trade show might do the trick. They asked Charlie to help find a trade show manager.

Charlie thought about who the ideal trade show producer for a new hardware show might be. After deliberation and conferring with his wife Virginia and his partner and brother-in-law, Bob Pomeranz, he came up with the answer: He would do it himself.

Charlie would be the show manager and producer of the first hardware show.

It would seem like an abrupt transition from his established law practice, but the prospect of a new business excited him. He would learn the fundamentals of shows from his hardware friends. Bob agreed to continue their partnership in an entirely different field.

It was a perfect fit for Charlie's easy smile and quick wit. He had a mind for business, and the courage to try something new. With his hardware manufacturer friends' support, he tackled the first event for the hardware industry at The Grand Central Palace in New York.

In 1980, while managing the National Hardware Show onsite at McCormick Place in Chicago, Charlie reminisced about the industry's inaugural event. In his show office after opening day, Charlie lit his favorite Cuban cigar. He held his perennial glass of vodka while he explained how The National Hardware Show got started.

He laughed and said the premier show had an endless list of things to do. One of the first was to create a show logo. Charlie said he remembered circus promoters beating a drum to build a crowd when they arrived in a new town. That enduring memory was the impetus for the drum becoming the National Hardware Show logo.

"The drum was our way of telling store owners and managers that the circus was in town. They could come to the big tent to meet and talk to 346 exhibitors at the show.

"The to-do list grew - meetings with hardware manufacturer friends who knew the market and their hardware store customers much better than Bob and I did. They were our Rosetta Stone, interpreting the needs of the industry, when and where to do the first show, and providing a lexicon of hardware jargon for our advertising copy. We were learning the business and tip-toeing through an entirely new vocabulary. We wanted to avoid embarrassment for ourselves or our hardware friends.

"We needed hardware industry publications to promote the new show, and we found out they needed us too. We were after exhibitors; they were after advertisers. We developed great symbiotic relationships with those editors and publishers. I can honestly say that together we built a thriving marketplace in print and an information network for our new industry.

"We were the new wave of marketing, and we acted as consumer advisors. The hardware retailers had to come and see what new products were on the market for the American consumer. It was a warehousing event to jumpstart their business – so they could stock their shelves for the coming selling season.

"With anything new, there are always some naysayers. It's human nature, I guess. Some retailers mistakenly expected their product line to stay the same year after year.

"But in 1946, the American economy was expanding; veterans coming back from the war had seen the world. They instinctively understood new products meant profit and growth. There was pent-up demand after World War II. Families were looking to fix up their homes, and new hardware and consumer products were becoming available on the market.

"We had a lot of new products in our first shows. Some were developed by the army during the war. New can openers, new drills, new oil cans, new towel racks, new shower heads. These were ready-made for housewives and husbands moving into new homes and apartments and needing to modernize their lives."

Charlie took a puff on his cigar and asked me to refill his glass of vodka.

"We showcased this venue at the Grand Central Palace. It had four floors and an open atrium in the center. Not a commodious place for a show. The freight elevators were too small. There were too many stairs. Union labor made exhibitors use their services. In spite of those shortcomings, we brought the industry together and had a great show. Exhibitors wrote orders. From the first day, the National Hardware Show proved to be a viable business.

"First-time exhibitors had faith in us, and we did not disappoint. When attendance was counted, we had 5,220 buyers from all over the United States. That was even before airline travel.

"Each year, more retailers understood what we were trying to do. They came back, show after show. They shopped the latest products, saw new vendors, swapped fresh ideas, and met old friends. Our show was really a catalyst for change. Hardware stores became convenience stores: stocking housewares, cooking utensils, home appliances, even kitchen sinks.

"We started a new show for hardware manufacturers that supported the growth of a billion-dollar industry. The old-fashioned hardware store with bins of nails and butcher aprons was replaced with inventory systems, bright lights, and shopping carts. We contributed to the way industry does business now. The biggest hardware chains in the world got their start about the same time as our show.

"This 1980 show will have 1,500 exhibitors and 30,000 hardware industry buyers. That's what happens when an industry gets behind an event. Black & Decker just said they wanted to expand their exhibit space. They have a new product line they want to introduce at our show. They are beating the drum for us now." Charlie beamed.

The gamble the hardware industry took of having Charlie and Bob run the show was providential. What it did for Charlie was profound:

he and his partner owned a show and a market that grew and prospered. They established a franchise in a main-stream American industry that was ultimately more valuable than their law practice. They no longer sought out clients. They were the client, and in a robust economy that kept their franchise growing year after year.

Charlie commented on his good fortune. "We never thought of ourselves as particularly trend-setting. We were simply workmen - providing a service the hardware industry said they needed. We took the same risks as any producer of any Broadway play: putting our money and our reputation on the line and hoping for the best.

We had good friends in the hardware industry who worked with us on that first show and made the transition to the business easy. It laid the groundwork for the continuation of our business in a lot of different shows.

"It provides a great sense of satisfaction that we contributed in some way to the enormous growth of the hardware industry. I'll be happy to have a drink to that!"

The current National Hardware Show (NHS) announced that the 75th anniversary event will take place October 2021 at the Las Vegas Convention Center, in Nevada. NHS anticipates a live trade show and the return of 25,000 industry professionals and 2,000 companies exhibiting, the show's statistical totals for the last live event in 2019. The NHS will continue to be the major event for the $345 billion U.S. home improvement and DIY markets.

Digital technology is revolutionizing the Accounting Show, currently an international forum in Australia, South Africa, Dubai, Singapore, Canada, and the United States.

7

The Accounting Show

Financial record keeping is as old as civilization. It existed in Meso-potamia in 10,000 BC. Double-entry bookkeeping, the current standard practice, was developed by Luca Pacioli in Italy in the 1500s. Accounting has become the indispensable requirement in business, finance, and government. My first show for Charlie was The Account-ing Show.

The president of the New York State Society of CPAs in 1974, was Eli Mason, a CPA visionary who championed small accounting firms. He wanted a show to bring technology and computer systems into the accounting profession. Computers were only used at that time by large firms. Eli wanted small firms to have the same computer capability. "CPAs are the nation's business doctors and they need computer technol-ogy to serve their clients better," he said.

Eli and Robert Gray (the Executive Director of the New York State Society of CPAs), wanted Charlie to manage the new show. They knew of his reputation with Coliseum events, including the New York Auto Show and the National Hardware Show. Charlie sent me to discuss their vision and confirm the deal.

When I told Charlie they wanted us to do their first show, he was elated. "Great news. Happy to have the New York State Society of CPAs onboard. You have my blessing to be the show manager."

This was an exciting career move in Charlie's company - managing a new show for New York's prestigious association of certified public accountants.

This was also an expansive time in my life. With two boys in tow, ages 4 and 2, and my wife active in her graphic design business, I was a

36-year-old with a career path in the trade show and exposition business. I had the experience, energy, and ambition to succeed in this fascinating business.

The first thing I learned was that my new CPA friends were an interesting breed. Super smart, disciplined, state-licensed like doctors and lawyers, they absorbed thousands of tax codes, legislative decrees, and client data to administer financial record-keeping and tax filing. As a non-CPA, my principal role was to listen and interpret arcane accounting terms into plain English for our promotional literature. Without hesitation, they reminded me that I was an acceptable messenger of CPA information, as long as I remembered I was not a CPA. As in ancient Greece, there were citizens and there were slaves. I was the latter, though quite useful as a scribe.

We had about nine months to put the show together. Primary requirements: come to terms with an agreement, pick a date (after the April 15 tax deadline), and select a hotel facility.

It surprised me a little that the CPAs were status-conscious about the show's location. In their minds, The New York Hilton was the only hotel that met their expectations. Occasionally, CPAs (who were the smartest and trendiest guys in the room), had opinions as undecipherable as their tax codes. We signed the contract, and the event was set for May 5-7, 1975, at the Hilton.

CPAs needed 120 CPE (Continuing Professional Education) credits over a three-year period to maintain their state CPA license. The Society would sponsor the conference with those credits.

New York CPAs in 1975 were office bound, and many were reluctant to attend a show during daytime billable hours. However, the incentive of low-cost CPE programs to learn about computers changed the minds of some old schoolers. Younger CPAs did not need encouragement. They understood the importance of computers. Many had already used them in college and MBA classrooms. The digital age had arrived. And since CPAs were required to pass stringent state exams and work for public CPA firms to qualify as certified public accountants, computers facilitated these mandates.

'One show has it all. One show does it all,' was the show's advertising theme - no hyperbole to offend CPA traditionalists. It was sufficient to draw in IBM, ADP, Paychex, and other major vendors to exhibit in the launch. We were successful in selling the concept to: banks, brokerage firms, tax preparation firms, calculator vendors, credit services, telephone systems, and office equipment suppliers.

Charlie reviewed progress at our traditional 5 o'clock drink and chat session.

"Make sure the show is worthwhile for the vendors as well as CPAs," Charlie said. "Make sure the Society gets top billing. They got to look good for their CPAs. And don't lose money."

The show would prove to be an impressive marketplace. IBM would introduce a new computer system; ADP, a new tax service; Paychex, a new payroll system. Exhibit sales picked up. Advance registration was active. The Society's conference was coming together. The Show Committee breathed a sigh of relief; the new event was generating interest and the potential revenue they had hoped for.

We had an inspired ally from the beginning. Eli Mason was a natural leader and wanted to be involved with every aspect of the show. He wanted to know how many exhibitors we had sold. He wanted to know how many CPAs we had registered. He wanted to know how many sleeping rooms we had reserved at the Hilton Hotel.

What made his interest doubly remarkable was that Eli suffered from the severe effects of *retinitis pigmentosa*, a genetic eye condition that caused complete blindness. It did not slow him down. His remarkable memory kept him in tune with every aspect of his CPA practice as well as the 1975 show.

The day before the kickoff, Eli and I met.

"So, how are the exhibitor payments going?" he asked. Eli was a financial wizard, and he always liked to anticipate the outcome of any transaction.

"Well, there's one exhibitor who keeps promising a check for $5,000, but has not yet delivered. But he assured me we'd get it today," I told him.

"Let me help," Eli offered. "I deal with theatrical people all the time and know about rubber checks. Tell this guy to give you the check today. If he waits until after 4 pm when the banks are closed, we'll fix him."

Surprise, surprise, when the exhibitor gave me his $5,000 check, it was after 4 pm and the bank had closed. True to his word, Eli went to work.

He called the bank and made sure they would stay open for his special messenger. The $5,000 check was delivered, and the money was immediately taken out of the exhibitor's account. This was accomplished by phone by Eli Mason, a legally blind CPA who became another personal friend and mentor.

The 1975 show was a resounding success with over 800 CPAs in attendance, surpassing prior attendance records for Society events. Exhibitors were pleased with the turn-out and wrote orders and promised to return in 1976. One exhibitor had a nice complaint/compliment. He couldn't meet the participant demand and ran out of literature.

So began a professional show for CPAs and their accounting vendors. The Accounting Show has energized the CPA market for digital systems, Internet, networks, online programs, finance services, and banking. It has become an essential forum for CPAs and their technology vendors in New York, Chicago, Los Angeles, Toronto, London, Melbourne, Sydney, Cape Town, Johannesburg, Dubai, and Singapore. In the United States, it serves 418,000 CPAs nationally and hundreds of thousands of Chartered Accountants throughout the world.

The event in 1975 confirmed the vital need for CPAs and their vendors to stay current. State-of-the-art companies have come along since, that have dramatically changed the landscape even further. In 1983, Intuit Corporation was founded by an innovator named Scott Cook. His firm is currently a U.S. $7 billion provider of accounting and tax preparation systems - just one example of the growth of the accounting marketplace.

My first show planted the seeds of a marketplace that continues to support a thriving digital accounting profession worldwide.

The New York Auto Show, a one-floor show at the New York Coliseum

8

The New York Auto Show –
A One-floor Show

The New York Automobile Show is the premier event of the automobile industry. The show started in 1900 and throughout its long history, embraced America's love of automobiles.

Snitow took the show over in the 1950s. Initially, it was held at the Grand Central Palace in midtown New York. The show then moved to the Coliseum at Columbus Circle in 1956 when the brand new, four-story, sparkling-white building was completed. Charlie still owned this multi-million-dollar event in 1978, and together with Jerry Martin, his long-time sales manager, nurtured it into the behemoth it became. (At the most recent live show in 2019, the Javits Center event had over one million visitors and 950,000 square feet of exhibit space. It was New York's largest public event.)

I had started with Charlie in 1974 and it would be my fourth Auto Show in 1978. Being on Charlie's team, I had become an old hand working to set-up and manage the show for every moment of its 8-day run, with its long public hours and throngs of car enthusiasts.

The Coliseum was always the place that General Motors, Ford, Chrysler, and all the other car makers came to for their annual Big Apple blitz. Detroit top brass would hold press conferences and private *tête-á-têtes* with their favorite editors and publishers. The show was their megaphone for news coming out of Detroit. The dailies published their stories and photos in special show supplements.

The show was on every manufacturer's event schedule as a have-to-be-there date. All except one year: 1978. That was the year the New York Automobile Show almost ceased to exist.

Detroit was stuck with indecision. They could not decide whether to introduce their cars in the spring or fall. The New York Auto Show was held in the fall.

Adding to the ambivalence towards committing, was the general tenor of the industry. *The New York Times* reported that family dealerships were being sold. Foreign manufacturers were flooding the market. Aggressive dealers were adding foreign makes. Some Detroit executives did not believe in the New York Show that year. Regional sales executives were being furloughed.

"Hi Jerry, we'd like to be with you, but to tell you the truth, I got my pink slip last week. I'm out the end of the month," a regional friend of Jerry Martin's reported. "I'd like to come to the show though, please send some tickets to my home address."

Also, show budgets were being cut. "Charlie, we've taken a new direction this year," one Detroit executive said. "We'll do the Detroit Auto Show because it's in our hometown. But we don't have the budget for New York."

Charlie conferred with Jerry. "What manufacturers do we have confirmed for our show this year?"

"We have Jaguar, Mercedes, Ferrari, Volvo, Peugeot, Alpha Romeo, Volkswagen, and many of the Japanese and Korean companies. But no Big Three," Jerry replied.

"You've got bubkis," Charlie said scornfully. "What the French call *Le concours d'Elegance*. A goddamn boutique. Not one Detroit manufacturer? We've got to do better than that or we'll be up the creek without a paddle."

Jerry was a former Marine and WW II veteran. He went to work as only he could, begging, sweet-talking, hornswoggling every car company from Stuttgart to Tokyo to Seoul. He earned his stripes and sold almost every non-Big Three manufacturer for the 1978 event.

The New York Auto Show was launched without a hint of the Big Three. Every New York TV station, newspaper, magazine, billboard, subway car, radio spot, and press release heralded the show. Local New York auto dealers were invited, and they, too, beat the drum for their New York car buyers.

"It's the Big Three's loss," Charlie said with resignation. "Detroit hasn't noticed that New York dealers really need the show. We'll get Detroit back," he said, "but we'll have to get through this year first." Charlie grew up in Hell's Kitchen, and he knew about survival. To some, it was his finest hour.

Jerry Martin finished selling his car manufacturers and determined the whole show could fit on one floor. There were four floors of the Coliseum available, but Charlie would only need the second floor. Without the Big Three's full line of cars, the show required much less space. The international manufacturers were all represented, but it was still only a skeleton of previous years.

A one-floor show.

The second floor had high ceilings, good lighting, and enough space for forty manufacturers. It was at the top of the escalators from the lobby level and glass entrance doors from Columbus Circle. Charlie's office was also on the second floor, and it was well stocked with Champagne, vodka, orange juice, bagels, lox, and cream cheese, for guests and staff for the entire eight days, as always.

Every aspect of the show was the same as in previous years. Same ribbon cutting. Same Champagne toasts in Charlie's office. Same crowds lining the sidewalks. Everything except the Big Three. The one-floor show was underway. Fortunately, the show had great weather and the crowds were as huge as ever.

Charlie Snitow was an impresario, and his one-floor show had some theatrical surprises. One was a songwriter who came in during set-up and offered to write a song to commemorate Charlie's 1978 show.

"Russell, give this man a drink, and show him around. We want to make our 'Director of Music' feel welcomed."

So it was, that our unpaid Director of Music joined our show management entourage. On the first evening of the event, to the tune of 'Another Op'nin Another Show,' our director and songwriter, played his original piece on his portable electronic keyboard at the top of the escalators at 6 pm.

He insisted Charlie, with his operatic baritone, and the entire show staff, join in singing the commemorative song. Attendees arriving up the

43

escalators were startled by this mixed singing chorus. Many were amused, others were mystified as they walked quickly past this impromptu entertainment. One man commented to his wife, "Just another car commercial, I guess."

"The song was not especially memorable, but was heartfelt," Charlie said with great generosity, smoking his cigar, and holding his plastic glass of Champagne. "You never know where you might find talent in this goddamn place. There's probably more talent on this one floor than in a Broadway play."

Charlie succeeded in having a great one-floor show in 1978. The attendance was as robust as in previous years. Attendees saw a new wave of international styling from import manufacturers. Exhibitors found customers for their new models. Charlie even made some money from the excellent attendance and income from the international exhibitors.

American car manufacturers resolved their spring and fall challenges and their budget crisis, and the Detroit Big Three came back with their complete line of cars in 1979. The New York Auto Show has continued to this day to be one of the most successful automobile shows in the world.

Charlie Snitow, with the sponsorship and support of the National Association of Specialty Food Trade (now the Specialty Food Association), launched The Fancy Food Show in 1955 at the Astor Hotel in New York.

9

The Fancy Food Show

Charlie was invited to lunch at Pappas Restaurant on 14th Street. It would be Snitow's first meeting with the National Association of Specialty Food Trade (NASFT). They knew him by reputation and wanted an experienced trade show producer to advise them on how to launch a new event. The year was 1954.

The NASFT was made up of importers and food purveyors headquartered in New York. Many were army veterans who had dined on delicious European and international cuisine and were eager to bring these items to the American consumer. (In celebrating 60 years of NASFT history, the association reported, "The 1950s brought a whole generation of men who had traveled overseas during World War II and returned with memories of culture and food they had never before experienced. Many formed importing companies to bring these fine food products to the U.S. market, where prosperity was beginning to make American tastes more supplicate.")

Then there were the international members who had long-established import businesses, retained their national pride, and had total distrust of other members in the import business. French importers had disdain for their German counterparts. Spanish importers did not think much of their Greeks competitors. Iranian caviar importers despised U.S. Hudson River caviar sellers. It wasn't unusual to hear native language invectives during shouting matches over a stolen retail grocery customer.

Importers and food purveyors were encouraging American retailers and their consumers to try new, and much more expensive, food and confection products. They were the supply chain to high-end specialty food shops, carriage-trade grocers, delicatessens, department stores, mail-order gift providers, and adroit retailers taking on European and international food products. Some importers were introducing 'fancy food and confections,' including tins of caviar from the Black Sea, containers of *foie gras* from France, elegant chocolates from Switzerland, sealed pouches of gravlax smoked salmon from Scotland, boxed dates and nuts from Morocco, and fancy tins of biscuits and tea products from England.

Now, new food and confection items were available for America's developing international tastes. Brie from France, feta from Greece, Bel Paese from Italy, and Limburger from Germany, were just a few of the cheeses offered at high-end food retail outlets. European wines were enticingly offered at every wine retailer for both family dining and neighborhood restaurants. Food had become a symbol of culture and status, and affluent Americans wanted the best for their personal consumption.

These gourmet food products were the hard-fought franchises of NASFT's fiercely combative members who looked to Charlie as a unifying force. They felt more comfortable with an impartial outsider. During the luncheon at Pappas (a classic West Side Greek restaurant with white linen table cloths and Victorian lighting sconces), Charlie shared how his trade shows had gotten started. He explained about The National Hardware Show and how he'd assembled the critical mass of vendors and buyers for the show. He described how NASFT members could do the same. After some negotiating, Charlie reached an agreement with the NASFT to manage their show.

Charlie quickly realized his biggest challenge was not the show itself, but getting these highly spirited competitors to work together. His engaging personality, confidence, and businesslike demeanor were repeatedly tested in luncheon meetings leading up to the show.

While Charlie and I shared our habitual 5 o'clock cocktail, he reminisced. "I remember meeting these guys who were at each other's throats. They were excellent receipt-counters and wanted to know what to expect from exhibit booth sales. To satisfy their concerns, I gave them a $7,500 figure in booth sales that I thought was conservative. My God, that was only $250 a booth back in 1955.

"Foods of France today [1978], spends $50,000 at the Summer Fancy Food Show alone and does not blink an eye.

"So, $7,500 sold these guys on working with me. They did not always get along with each other, but they got along famously with me. I was neutral and could adjudicate their squabbles with a voice of reason. I was their judge and jury. I loved it.

"Just before the first show, we had a final meeting, and I reminded these guys, 'You are all men of good will, and you will have to work together to make the first time show successful.' And they did."

"Working with the NASFT was a match made in heaven. It was good for them and good for me. The first Fancy Food and Confection Show at the Astor Hotel in Times Square was "an unbelievably great success," in the words of one of NASFT's founders, Al Cook. It was propitious that this new event coincided with America's new palate for imported and specialty foods. Our timing was perfect."

Like many of Charlie's first-time events, the show began modestly. There were 82 booths and 524 in attendance, but that was the critical mass Charlie was looking for. They were the prime sellers and buyers in the emerging food marketplace, and 50 importers of specialty foods became new members of NASFT after seeing their retailers shopping the trade show for new imported products.

"The conditions were right for that first show in August of 1955. We had fancy food retailers, specialty food shops, wholesale and gift providers, and their vendors. The Astor Hotel in Times Square was a great venue for the kick-off.

"We were pioneers back then. Food purveyors were finding their niche with the American consumer. I was finding my niche with new shows. We never dreamed the Fancy Food and Confection Shows would become the mainstream events they are today. But we had trust in each other, and we had trust in the American market. Our first show did over $1 million in business."

An editorial in *Telefood Magazine* in October 1955, reported on the first show: "There were some who thought labeling the show "First Annual" was unnecessarily optimistic. Let there be no doubt about it, there will be a "Second Annual" and many more. We are proud of our own part in the show and that we were there in the beginning."

Snitow guided NASFT through the first 25 years of the show. Together they launched shows on the east and west coasts. These have flourished since 1955, becoming two annual, multi-million-dollar events: one in New York at the Javits Center - The Summer Fancy Food Show; the second in San Francisco at the Moscone Center -The Winter Fancy Food Show.

These two 1978 major events were showcases for imported and domestic food products of the world. They featured elaborate country pavilions, including: 'Foods of France,' 'Foods of Germany,' 'Foods of Spain,' and other country-sponsored exhibits. These two shows were the United Nations of food, with elaborate and exotic country offerings from Asia, Africa, South America. Both shows were must-attend-events for wholesalers, major retailers, and specialty buyers of international foods and confections. The NASFT importers were still there, but The Fancy Food Show had become a world-class emporium and not a clublike boutique exclusively for the original New York members.

These shows had miles of aisle carpeting; elaborate and stunning booths with refrigerated display cases for cheeses, meats, and perishables; attractive models and company personnel who sometimes dressed in their native costumes; samples of every type of food and confection. It should be noted that the caviar purveyors did not offer free tastings. Instead, they provided a printed product description with a complete guide to the size of eggs with each category of caviar. Even in the greatest food show on earth, there are some purveyors that did not give away free samples.

Eventually, NASFT took over the shows when Charlie retired. But he is not forgotten. He was elected posthumously to the Specialty Food Association (the modern name of the NASFA), Hall of Fame in 2016. The commemoration read:

> "Charlie Snitow was a creator of the modern trade show after World War II. A tough negotiator and conciliator, he brought together competitors, labor, and management, often over fine food, drinks and cigars."

SHOT is the largest annual firearms exhibition in the world. The 42nd Annual event held in Las Vegas, boasted over 2,000 exhibitors and 61,000 attendees from 50 states and 100 international countries.

10

The SHOT Show

Rocky Rohlfing was not a rich factory owner.
Members of the National Shooting Sports Foundation (NSSF) were. Rocky was their salaried association executive working out of a small, second-floor office in Riverside, Connecticut. He was wheelchair bound, but he had a vision. Rocky had the wild idea of hosting a NSSF trade show.

He knew his NSSF arch-conservative members and doubted they would be enthusiastic about a show. On the other hand, Rocky felt a trade show would generate income and customers for his manufacturers. His idea led him to Charlie Snitow's office to discuss a show for gun retailers to meet NSSF gun manufacturers.

Rocky educated Charlie about how the NSSF members had a celebrated history as far back as the Civil War and the Wild West. Remington, Winchester, Colt, and others, had provided pistols and rifles since the beginning of the American Industrial Revolution when machine-made, interchangeable parts were introduced. They were the armorers of the U.S. military and the gunmakers of the pioneers, hunters, and cattlemen, who tamed the American West.

NSSF members valued their place in history. Commemorative pistols and rifles were often given to U.S. presidents who became personal friends. They were essential players contributing to the expansion of the United States.

Charlie understood Rocky's goals were similar to those of his National Hardware Show and other dealer-oriented shows under his management. Unlike the New York Auto Show (open to the general public, with attendees buying an admission ticket to attend), the SHOT would be a private event, open only to the gun trade. Dealers would need to register and obtain a badge credential to attend. Charlie was confident he could help. He knew what worked for dealers; Rocky knew what worked for gun manufacturers. Charlie would produce the first event sponsored by NSSF, and Jerry Van Dyke was brought in to manage the show.

A huge task lay before Jerry. He had to convince rock-ribbed, Yankee mill owners to spend their money on Rocky's show. Those guys lived by the word parsimonious. They could not understand why their association even needed a show. Many owned yachts and attended boat shows, but in their opinion, gun shows were for collectors and hobbyists, not serious gun manufacturers.

Jerry and Rocky had to convince NSSF members to exhibit, otherwise there would be no event. Slowly, Remington, Colt, and other NSSF members came onboard though they questioned their investment in the show. Other gun manufacturers were confirmed, as well as shooting, hunting, and outdoor sports exhibitors. The Shooting, Hunting, and Outdoor Trade Show - SHOT - was beginning to take shape.

Next, Jerry and Rocky turned their attention to gun retailers. They put together advertising, promotion, and PR, and with the help of gun and outdoor sports publications, invited retailers and gun sellers to attend. It would be held at the St. Louis Convention Center in January, 1979.

The SHOT was a resounding success, even with Rocky Rohlfing's memorable opening comment, "Well boys, I hope someone shows up." Over 200 gun and sporting goods exhibitors and 5000 dealers participated. Many NSSF members were relieved that the show even took place.

Three years later, in 1982, I became the show manager of the SHOT. Although the composition of it was already changing, I chose an Audubon duck stamp print for the cover of the show directory. It was a mallard duck in full flight, emphasizing wildlife, hunting, and outdoor sports. For me, it defined firearms as a recreational activity of American life. Exhibitors that year had shotguns for bird shooting, rifles for deer hunting, pistols for target shooting. However, firearms manufacturers were also responding to gun owners wanting rapid-fire weapons. That was the beginning of SHOT as a Second Amendment event for military weapons buyers.

One of the intriguing military items that year was a sniperscope that could find a target by starlight at 1500 yards. Sniper scopes are normally not used for deer hunting by starlight from almost a mile away. What had boosted demand for military-style weapons were army veterans desiring and familiar with rapid-fire AR 15s and citizens wanting a weapon for a greater sense of security in their lives. The recent movie, *American Sniper,* portrayed a Navy Seal with a sniper scope killing an Iraqi Jihadist at 1500 yards. That sniper scope was an example of the kind of weapon and component that had become commonplace at SHOT.

The growth of SHOT has been exponential since 1982. NSSF no longer needs a benign duck stamp on its directory cover for its marketplace for AR and AK firearms, high-capacity magazines, assault weapons, camouflage clothing, silencers, sniper scopes, knives, and electronic combat games. Its membership has also increased, and NSSF has a government relations office in Washington, D.C., similar to the National Rifle Association, to advise Congress on gun legislation.

Charlie Snitow and Jerry Van Dyke retired from Reed in the late 1980's, after shepherding SHOT through its first decade. In 2012, Reed resigned from the SHOT after the Sandy Hook Elementary School massacre in Newtown, Connecticut. The show is currently managed by NSSF, and their headquarters are now located in Newtown. Their office is 100 times larger than Rocky's Riverside office.

In 2013, SHOT was held at the Las Vegas-Sands Convention Center, just 60 days after, and 2 miles from, the massacre of concertgoers by the rapid-fire shooter with a bump stock, firing from the 32nd floor of the Mandalay Bay Hotel.

The 2020 SHOT (the 42nd), also held at The Sands Convention Center, hosted the fourth largest show in Vegas with 630,000 square feet of space. It was the 25th largest show in the United States, boasting 2,000 exhibitors and 61,000 attendees coming from 50 states and 100 international countries. (That is the combined population of Greenwich and Riverside, Connecticut, where Rocky had his first office.) SHOT is now the largest show for personal assault weapons in the world.

Rocky's vision was far-reaching, but he could not have imagined a show of such proportion or complexity. The first SHOT had mom-and-pop gun shops and retail-chain buyers with specialty hunting and fishing departments. The 2020 SHOT had a vastly different audience. Gun buyers were mass retailers, international arms dealers, and security and police organizations from around the world. Mom-and-pop gun shops still attended, but they sell AR 15's.

Further, a *Wall Street Journal* article reporting on the 2020 SHOT, revealed an intended expansion of its customer-base. The headline read: 'Gunmakers Adjust Focus for Women Buyers.' It stated that the nation's gun trade had identified women as the new target market for handguns for personal protection. Gun-ready fashions were being shown at the SHOT with a new line of women's apparel to accommodate concealed weapons. Women can now pack a pistol in classrooms, churches, offices, and Stop and Shop.

The 2020 SHOT has taken America to an alternate universe for Second Amendment advocates and the world market for automatic weapons. It started in Charlie Snitow's office in 1978.

The American Toy Association's Toy Fair fills the Javits Center's annual event with 8 football fields of exhibit space, 30,000 toy retailers, and 1,038 exhibitors.

11

The Tempestuous Start
of the Great American Toy Fair

This story reflects the enduring Broadway motto: "The Show Must Go On." The American Toy Association phoned Charlie and wanted to do a new show. The ATA already had a successful Toy Fair founded 75 years previous in 1903 for members. Eager to capture the rapidly expanding American toy market, they wanted Snitow to launch an additional show for non-members, including Asian and European toy makers, that would run in tandem with their established event.

The ATA's Toy Fair was not a show per se, but an open house, held annually in February, at their headquarters and show rooms at Madison Square Park and West 24th Street in New York. Mattel, Tonka, Hasbro, and other major American members were exhibitors. It was geared towards buyers from toy stores, big box stores, department stores, and mass merchandisers. The hottest new toys were showcased: Star Wars light sabers, Tonka steel toy trucks, Barbie and Ken dolls, and electronic board games.

Anticipating tremendous growth in the industry, the ATA recognized the need to bring non-members and new toy makers to a stand-alone Midtown hotel show. They wanted Charlie's expertise and reputation behind it. They did not know that Charlie's carefully hewn trade show shop had evolved into a Harvard Business School model enterprise

Charlie's show business had reached its 21st year in 1977. He had sold his company to Reed Publishing in 1965 and was working side-by-side with Bob Krakoff since 1975, Bob being the co-president installed by Reed Publishing. Bob was responsible for new business and he jumped at the chance to start a show for the prestigious American Toy Association.

Bob appointed the new vice president he had just hired, Tom O'Rourke, to run it (a fellow Harvard Business School graduate though from their summer executive program). He had little experience in trade shows, but was a quick study. Tom's previous job was with a credit card company as vice president of merchant services. This would be his first trade show.

The Sheraton Hotel on West 53rd Street and Seventh Avenue was selected as the site for Tom's Great American Toy Fair, the new name to differentiate it from The Toy Fair. The hotel, an ideal location, was one of the most popular and convenient midtown meeting sites in Manhattan. Albert Hall would be their exhibit hall, located in the sub-basement. Although not apparent to anyone other than a civil engineer, its underground location was adjacent to subways lines, water mains, gas, electric, and communication lines, and the entire infrastructure that coursed under every street and building in Manhattan. In other words: Albert Hall was literally inches from some of the most potent dangers in the city.

Tom was a gifted salesperson with the charm of an Irish peddler. As a former baseball player, he loved the rough and tumble of competition. He and his team went to work and succeeded in selling Czech doll manufacturers, German miniature car producers, Taiwanese board game developers, Korean electronics makers, and American non-ATA members. While there were no Mattels, Hasbros, or Tonkas, the new companies were eager to exhibit at the Sheraton that February.

Tom's event might be called a 'rump' show in trade show parlance. But it was an excellent first-time sales effort all the same. His three-day show was scheduled to open Sunday and continue Monday and Tuesday.

On Saturday night, a giant winter snowstorm blasted New York City.

The show was completely set up, ready for the Sunday morning opening. By 7 PM Saturday, Midtown streets were completely flooded. The tempestuous rain and snow overwhelmed the city's sewer systems everywhere – and especially around West 53rd Street and 6th Avenue, on every side of the Sheraton Hotel!

Albert Hall, being in the sub-basement, was a bathtub without a drain. One of the adjacent water mains burst, and water cascaded like a waterfall into the exhibit hall. In an hour, everything was inundated, completely submerging: set-up exhibitor displays, carpeting, new toy samples, and elegant electronic signage. The electricity had to be shut off to prevent electrocution for those wading in the hall. Damage was overwhelming.

Tom and his crew were staying in the hotel and immediately were alerted to the flood. Rushing to Albert Hall, they worked (together with hotel staff), all night, desperate to save their show. By morning, they had mopped, squeegeed, and drained most of the water from the show floor. Attendees walking the event on Sunday morning were startled by the squishing sound underfoot and their wet shoes.

Yet Tom's first show achieved some success despite the flood. Exhibitors met prospects and wrote orders. Attendees were introduced to new toy suppliers. Tom arranged for the following year's dates, in 1979, to again be held in Albert Hall. He apologized to all and promised a better show. (His learning curve was complete. The show continued successfully.)

Charlie was surprisingly taciturn in regards to Krakoff's new show. Perhaps the American Toy Association show had less champagne and camaraderie and more Harvard Business School scripture. Not ungenerous, though, he applauded Tom O'Rourke's major-league effort to save the first annual Great American Toy Fair from the flooded sub-basement of the Sheraton Hotel.

In 1985, The ATA brought Snitow's Great American Toy Fair in-house and integrated it into their Toy Fair at the Javits Convention Center as one giant, sold-out show.

The explosive growth of toy retailing represents a $27 billion industry today. The 2019 Toy Fair at the Javits Center covered 8 football fields of exhibit space. There were 30,000 toy retailers at the show, 98 countries represented, and 1,038 exhibitors participated. The world's top online and brick and mortar retailers attended, including Amazon, Wal-Mart, Target, Kohl, Costco, Best Buy, Walgreens, and Disney Stores, among others. Motion picture and streaming film producers also participated, including Netflix, Disney, Marvel, Sesame Street, Warner Bros, NBC Universal, and Amazon. Hollywood and the giants of the toy industry have now merged with increasingly popular events like Comicon and

Comic Book Expo, with tens of thousands of attendees drawn to each event.

The cascading deluge that almost ruined the Great American Toy Fair is an example of the calamity that can face any live event. Charlie understood that reality.

"You roll the dice and take your chances. Experience helps, but no one can prevent a waterfall or some other disaster. You just have to suck it up and solve the problem if it occurs. No one told Tom what to do, but he was instinctive, and his crew did a great job of saving the toy show. That's what our business is all about."

The Greater New York Automobile Dealers Association manages and produces the premier Greater New York International Auto Show annually at the Javits Center. It is the largest annual public-attended event in New York. In 1976, Charlie Snitow produced the Auto Show with a masterful response to multiple bomb threats.

12

"I'm Not Kidding This Time"

Bomb threats are a way of life.

The New York Post headlines announce bomb threats as an everyday occurrence. Bomb threats are meant to disrupt and terrorize. It was especially true at the New York Automobile Show in 1976 at the Coliseum.

The Auto Show was the most attended public event at the Coliseum that year. The venue had opened nine years earlier in 1957, at the site of the present Time Warner twin towers. The Coliseum was the largest and most modern exhibition facility at the time, and had four floors of exhibition space, a parking garage underneath, and a subway station outside at West 58th Street and Columbus Circle.

Thousands of New Yorkers were already gathered that Easter Saturday morning inside the Coliseum waiting for the show to open. Exhibitors, fashion models, ticket ushers, security guards, and NYPD officers were already inside at their assigned places. More than 500,000 visitors were expected over the eight-day event, eager to see the new cars from the United States and around the world. Fifty thousand attendees were expected on the opening Saturday alone. The sun was shining. Spring was in the air. Families were dressed in their Easter Sunday best. The lobby was overflowing with the excited crowd. The parking garage was filled. The subway station was packed. New crowds were arriving on every train.

Charlie Snitow presided over the ribbon cutting, with the *New York Post* photographer at the ready. Dignitaries included Mayor Abe Beame, a Governor Rockefeller staffer, New York Auto Dealers Association officers, top executives from Ford and Chevy, and New York dealer friends. After the photo-op, the whole group assembled in Charlie's office on the second floor for the traditional Champagne toast.

The tiny office was stocked with a weekend's supply of Champagne, fresh orange juice, warm bagels, lox, cream cheese, and an open bar. Charlie's guests crowded in and were all poised with their plastic glasses filled with Champagne, ready for the toast.

"Let's drink to open the show," Charlie beamed.

More Champagne flowed and glasses were filled again. "Here's to a great show!" Charlie toasted. "We set a new record with the Japanese this year. Drink up. There is more where that came from."

The next day, at 3 pm, the phone rang in Charlie's office.

It was the Coliseum switchboard operator.

"Mr. Snitow?" Her voice was tight with panic. "We've just received a terrifying call – there's a bomb in the building! The caller said it's timed to go off in 15 minutes! What should I do?"

Charlie immediately called Howard Persina, the building manager on his radio. "Come to my office right away, Howard. It's an emergency."

After conferring with Persina, Charlie called the NYPD. He calmly spoke to the local precinct commander, who said he'd call downtown and call right back.

Two minutes later, Charlie got the call.

"Stay in the building at your own risk. But we recommend you evacuate," the commander said.

"What should we tell the crowd? There are probably at least 30,000 people here!"

"Simply say the building must be evacuated for 'security reasons.' Don't say why, and for God's sake, don't say bomb," the commander advised. "The bomb squad has been dispatched."

"We've got to go," Charlie said to Howard, as calm as ever. "Get on the PA and let the guards and NYPD know right away. We can't have anyone hurt. Russ, go down to the lobby with the bull horn to help get the crowds out the glass doors to the street."

"What a city," he lamented. "This is all we need."

Evacuating the four-floor Coliseum with thousands of people of all ages was daunting and dangerous. Making the situation even more tenuous was the unreliable Coliseum public address system. The show guards, the NYPD, and Charlie's staff were learning how to evacuate the huge building for the first time.

I was in the lobby with an electronic bull horn, providing constant safety announcements to calm the enormous crowd as they slowly passed by.

"Please stay calm and proceed through the glass doors to the street," I directed. "Make sure to have your wrist stamped on the way out. We promise you'll be back in the show shortly." Rubber stamps were given to security guards who took on the task of stamping wrists.

Families, kids, exhibitors, everyone was on the move. Down the stairways, down the elevators, down the escalators, out the glass doors, onto the sidewalk at West 58th Street and Columbus Circle. Many didn't hear the PA. Some were startled and confused. Older people in wheelchairs and walkers were challenged and slow. Lost kids and missing parents were everywhere. Remarkably, no one was injured. No one panicked. It was inspiring - like watching a slow-moving train with a steady flow of passengers oozing out of the building. Every inch of sidewalk around the Coliseum, from West 58th Street to Columbus Circle was filled with attendees. The crowd remained orderly. Some thought it some kind of promotion.

The NYPD had arrived immediately with their dogs, and the bomb squad searched each floor. They checked trash containers, empty crates, and obvious places that might hide a bomb. After 45 minutes, no devices were found. The phone caller had said '15 minutes.'

A lieutenant and his sergeant came into Charlie's office wearing flak jackets and helmets after the search. "We didn't find any devices, sir. Could be just a 'reasonable threat.' Crank callers are part of our life nowadays."

"Should we bring them back?" Charlie asked soberly. "Are you telling me there are no explosives?"

"No guarantee, sir. But I'd say it's a probable 'okay.' It's your call though. It's your show," the lieutenant said.

"Okay," Charlie said with a resigned sigh. "Bring them back, and tell the guards they need show tickets or wrist stamps."

The doors reopened and the crowd surged in. In truth, it was impossible to check stamped wrists with thousands returning. The crowd was in a good mood though. Charlie's staff, security guards, and NYPD welcomed them back with smiles. No explanation was given.

"Can't say, ma'am," one officer offered in response to why people had to leave the show. "Just security, I guess." 'Just security,' was the only explanation for the entire eight days.

The same or different callers phoned the Coliseum 16 more times during the eight days of the show. The building was evacuated 17 times: Mornings. Afternoons. Twice in one evening. On the last Sunday, the bomb caller phoned again.

The Coliseum switchboard called Charlie and repeated what the caller said.

"I'm not kidding this time."

The Auto Show evacuated the Coliseum more times than any other show that year. Down the escalators, down the stairs, down the elevators, through the marble lobby, out the glass doors, onto the sidewalk 17 times. There were no lawsuits. There were no refunds. Just another Auto Show.

"In all my years in this business," Charlie said, on Sunday evening when the event was over, "this was the most memorable show we've ever had. Let's have a drink to close the show. And let's get that damn lieutenant in here to have a drink, too!"

Charlie Snitow advised a major trade show producer in Brazil on his annual Sao Paulo International Auto Show.

13

Caio Machado and the Sao Paulo International Auto Show

Caio Machado came to New York with a problem. He needed Charlie Snitow's help.

A longtime friend of Charlie's, Caio was a major producer of trade shows in Sao Paulo, Brazil. He became my friend, too, after long lunches with Charlie at Sniffin Court.

A large man with a voracious love of life, Caio relished food and fine wine. Sitting down to pizza (the unofficial national dish of Brazil), he'd say, "This whole pie is just the right size for my appetite!" His entourage always included a bevy of attractive women. Charlie and he shared a delight in the pleasures of the world.

Alcantara Machado Ltda. was Caio's company and the producer of the Sao Paulo International Auto Show, annually held in November. Caio owned the show and ran it with the Brazilian Automobile Manufacturers Association that included Ford, GM, Volkswagen, and others Brazilian carmakers, manufacturing and selling exclusively to the domestic Brazilian market.

The Sao Paulo Convention Center was the site of Caio's event, the largest automobile show in South America. It attracted over a million attendees. It was Sao Paulo's answer to the New York Auto Show, but with styling and performance trends tailored to the Brazilian consumer, with all cars of Brazilian origin.

With a vintage Bordeaux in hand, Caio explained his situation.

"Charlie, here's the problem: every Brazilian manufacturer has balked at exhibiting in my show. They say they've blown their 1987 budgets for the year – can't afford another November show. They complain that Brazilian inflation has hammered car sales and other luxury purchases.

"These are my friends – we belong to the same clubs, eat at the same fine restaurants. They're still flush, but all I hear are apologies and regrets. 'Sorry, Caio, we cannot join you this year.'

"And Charlie, you know I can't bring in any international car imports - I'm still restricted by the government. My exhibitors have to be Brazilian manufacturers."

Charlie listened attentively, nodding his head as he took in the conundrum. He thrived on problem solving.

"I think I know who can help you," Charlie said.

This story has a twist and a new character. Enter Stephen Cox, a clever and longtime employee of Charlie's. Steve was a fixture and a knowledgeable facilitator for Charlie at the New York Automobile Show.

Charlie also suggested Caio contact Charlie's New York international bank to secure a bridge loan for approximately 2 million dollars. After an introduction, his banker was only too happy to make the collateralized loan for Charlie's wealthy friend from Brazil.

Caio, Charlie, Steve, and their banker, worked out a grand plan to resuscitate the November show in Sao Paulo. Here is the inside story of their amazing collaboration: they would provide cars for the 1987 show that could not be provided by Brazilian car manufacturers. Their strategy would bypass Brazilian carmakers altogether and still produce a phenomenal event for Sao Paulo and its car aficionados.

Caio would import cars from the United States. His Brazilian public would see amazing new models for the first time from the U.S., Europe, and Asia, that they had only read about or seen on television. And how would Brazilian import restrictions remain intact? The cars would not be sold in Brazil.

As always, Caio saw this enormous undertaking in simple terms and as a game he could play on his stubborn, rich manufacturing friends. At the same time, his event would be on every newspaper's front page, every TV station's news program, and every business and entertainment calendar of events.

A wily operator who spent his whole life navigating around Brazilian government regulations, economic upheavals, and normal everyday chaos, Caio's delicious response to the boycott was his stunning jewel-box of international automotive manufacturers under the noses of his carmaker friends. They could only sniff with envy.

Caio was from one of Brazil's most prestigious families. He knew how to preserve status and wealth. He also knew a calmer time would come when he would prevail and continue his auto show with Brazilian manufacturers in 1988. He had to get through 1987 first.

Steve was a key player in Caio's mission to select and buy the finest representation of new cars that U.S. dealers had to offer at the lowest, negotiated price. The cars had to be stunning and exemplify the latest styling and glamour that Detroit, Stuttgart, Tokyo, and Seoul, had in 1987. They had to wow a discriminating South American car-viewing public.

Sao Paulo is Brazil's largest and most sophisticated city, with a population of over 20 million. Sao Paulistanos are taste-makers in art, music, fashion, business, and consumer goods. They expect to see the finest products from the most elite retailers of the world at their fashion malls and exclusive shops. Likewise, their automobile show has to have the same high bar of excellence.

Steve had to be ready each morning to accompany Caio to auto showrooms around New York. Steve said Caio was a magic genie who could open doors and flatter dealers with his Portuguese accent and gracious Brazilian charm. The job was a magical plum, too.

There would be an obligatory two-hour break for luncheon at one of Caio's favorite New York destinations, whether '21,' *La Cote Basque*, or another fine restaurant. Then an afternoon drive to several showrooms the industry refers to as 'stores.'

Each store had its own delights. Handsome glass-enclosed car displays, spotless tile floors, dramatic lighting, and gracious owner/dealers with afternoon treats of champagne, freshly brewed coffee, finger food, and desserts. Store meetings, Steve observed, felt like British royalty visiting village shopkeepers.

They checked out almost every major dealership in New York and Connecticut. From 10th Avenue in New York, to Queens Boulevard, then Westchester, and finally, Connecticut. They were two of the most welcomed shoppers at every store. The dealers could tell they had money when they walked through the door. They had the financial firepower, but they needed enough cars to fill the Sao Paolo Convention Center. The $2 million budget would only take them so far.

Each car had to be selected, negotiated, and purchased at Caio's special discounted dealer price. Arrangements had to be made to deliver each vehicle to the Port of Newark to be loaded on to a seagoing car carrier for shipment by ocean freight to a port in Brazil and then overland to Sao Paolo. Cars had to be prepped for ocean travel. Export documentation had to be executed. This arduous procedure was repeated with each car.

Before the show even took place in Brazil, the United States logistics of Caio's strategy was the equivalent of preparing for a D-Day invasion. Steve and Caio had experts working with them every step of the way, but anxiety was still a constant. Would every car arrive in Sao Paulo in the same condition it left the Port of Newark?

All cars shipped into Brazil were designated bonded goods, and none could be sold inside Brazil. The Convention Center became a bonded warehouse. The cars were crown jewels to be admired but not worn.

Caio was an old hand at car shows. His event was lavished with every elegant accoutrement: deep pile carpeting, dramatic stage lighting, turntables, beautiful models, live music, electronic signage, and ribbon cutting with the mayor, governors, and dignitaries, including his manufacturing friends.

The consummate host, Caio made sure his rich friends and his car manufacturer CEOs received special invitations to his opening Champagne reception. He was a showman at heart, and this American extravaganza was his finest hour. At the show, over a million Sao Paulo car lovers previewed 50 splendid automobiles they could never buy in a Brazilian showroom. Brazilian car worshipers went gaga over models with the latest automotive design, including T-Birds, Corvettes, Cadillacs, Mercedes, and Toyotas.

A final perk for Steve Cox was being invited down to see the result of their shopping spree. "It was the New York Auto Show on steroids," he said, "except in Portuguese. The only thing missing were retail sales. The show was fantastic and achieved a rare '10' in a discriminating city not given over to American superlatives."

However, for anyone who has spent time at auto shows, it is understood that two weeks of exhibiting creates extraordinary wear and tear on cars. Seats, steering wheels, interiors, become shopworn. Unconscionable attendees steal operating equipment and accessories and consider the show an auto parts warehouse. Some cars simply became inoperable after two weeks of Sao Paulo show traffic.

The final logistics were an interesting coda to the event. At the conclusion, Caio's cars had to be reloaded on car carriers for ocean freight back to the United States. Though the cars were bought new and still had worth, the $2 million had a depreciation that only the Atlantic Ocean and Sao Paulo show visitors could extract from a car's showroom value.

Yet Caio more than offset his show expenses, including his bridge loan and its depreciation, with his attendance gate revenue. He was able to resell all of his cars at a reasonable price, even after some needed refurbishing or replacement parts. Of greater significance, Caio was the wizard able to welcome back all of his Brazilian manufacturing friends in 1988.

Ultimately, Caio's firm was acquired by Reed Exhibitions, the same British RELX Corporation that acquired Charlie's company. Caio continued coming to New York, and my finest memories were joining him at '21' while he decided how to satisfy his enormous appetite. The Sao Paulo International Auto Show continues to this day.

Jerry Jordan provided services at the 8th Annual CES that included a Cadillac limousine.

14

The Chicago Limousine

In 1975, the 8th Annual Consumer Electronics Show was held, and Charlie Snitow and Jack Wayman presided over it with pride. Having grown into a twice-a-year event, the winter show was put on at the original location at the Chicago Hilton, and a summer show was featured at McCormick Place, Chicago.

Exhibitor budgets for the summer CES were enormous. Panasonic, Sony, Motorola, GE, NEC, and others, spent hundreds of thousands of dollars on two-story exhibits, private hospitality suites, and special parties, all to sell to the 30,000 CES retailers attending.

Chicago service contractors, appointed by Charlie and Jack on an annual basis, were the benefactors of this bonanza. They and their huge workforces were recipients of this windfall generated through the expansive growth of CES. The winning contractors could count on bragging rights and a huge payday after two weeks of work. Competition was fierce to win the CES appointments.

One of the newest Chicago contractors competing that year was Jerry Jordan. He grew up in Chicago and earned his chops in labor and business. He was in the rug business. He was in the pizza business. He had Chicago "boss" connections. Jerry was gregarious, athletic, and funny. He knew his way around executive offices, athletic clubs, and freight docks.

Jerry's bid for CES in 1975 was unsuccessful. However, competitive and a games player, he had incentive and a brilliant idea. When Charlie and Jack arrived at O'Hare for the 1975 show, Jerry was there to meet them. After a welcoming greeting, with a magnanimous smile on his face,

Jerry presented them with the use of a brand new, Cadillac limousine and a young driver who knew Chicago.

He then made a promise to the trade show producers: "There are absolutely no strings attached."

Knowing a bribe when they saw it, Charlie and Jack expressed themselves accordingly. "Sorry Jerry, we don't need your limousine."

Jerry's response was classic Jerry. "It's already leased. I can't take it back. Just take it and use it. I guarantee there are no strings."

Charlie and Jack paused, which was unusual for these worldly men. Their pause was followed by: "Oh well, if you can't return it, we'll use it just now and again."

And use it they did - constantly - during the entire two weeks. They were driven back and forth by limousine to McCormick, Chicago hotels, and evening soirées to Chicago restaurants. If someone needed a flip chart, the limousine was available. Transportation was not a luxury, but a necessity in Chicago. Thanks to Jerry, this efficient and convenient (and opulent), mode of travel was on call at CES for the duration of the show.

The Chicago limousine was the entrée Jerry needed to ingratiate himself with Charlie and Jack. No reminder to use it was needed; it was indispensable. Likewise, he offered himself as a Chicago friend and guide. If they wanted a new restaurant, he had the perfect spot to recommend. If they needed to buy shoes, he pointed them to the best discount shoe store in the city. Jerry was in their company for the entire two weeks. At dinners, parties, and at CES. A wonderful camaraderie was established between the three of them.

After the show closed, visits to Charlie's New York office commenced. Jerry made sure Jack was in New York when he visited Charlie, and he built rapport with Charlie's managers. Jerry understood labor from the union hiring hall to the freight docks and continued as their unpaid advisor.

A few of the "bosses" he knew were occasionally reported on in *The Tribune*, and he once confessed that his own mother worked for an important one. Jerry helped Charlie and Jack negotiate service agreements, invaluably saving them money.

Not surprisingly, the next year, Jerry won his coveted contractor bid for CES. The Chicago limousine and driver had served Jerry well in 1975, and he brought them back in 1976. This boon became part of Jerry's service.

In addition to serving as an official contractor for CES, he was engaged for the same function at all of Charlie's shows. His company was honest and gave the exhibitors a fair shake. He became Charlie's go-to guy. Jerry made his money as an official contractor, yet ceaselessly offered additional gratis contributions. He was the genie in the bottle, willing to do everything for Charlie and Jack to make their lives easier. And true to his word, he was careful not to ask for anything in return. But he knew they appreciated his services.

Jerry became my friend too, and in addition to his impact on Charlie's bottom line, it was his personality and generosity that made us appreciate him. Often, his office visits were like Catskill Borscht Belt comedy routines. Jerry was a master storyteller. He was Jewish, as was Charlie and Jerry Martin, and his jokes usually had a Yiddish punch line. The whole office became Jewish for a day, understanding the hilarity of Jerry's Yiddish humor.

As a goy (gentile man), or shiksa (gentile woman), we goyim (non-Jews), grew accustomed to Yiddish as a second language in the office. Terms of endearment like bubeleh (darling boy), or derision, like schmuck (jerk), flowed freely. We quickly understood who the machers (capable doers), were and who were the kvetchers (complainers). We learned about chutzpah (courage), meshugas (nonsense), nosh (snack), and bubkes (emphatically nothing), as part of our everyday talk. It was not a mitzvah (good deed), to speak Yiddish, it was just a shtick (habit), when making conversation.

One of Jerry's greatest pleasures was finding new places to eat in New York. One such treasure was Sammy's Roumanian Restaurant on Chrystie Street on the lower East Side. Located in a tenement basement, it was loud, had music and dancing, and old-style waiters. One Monday evening, Jerry invited Charlie, Jack Wayman, Jerry Martin, Betty Djerf, Steve Cox, and me, to join him there. After Jerry assembled his guests at a grand table, he announced, "Welcome to my new home. This place is not for calorie counters. We're here to destroy you goyim."

Tables were set with tubs of pickles and peppers and small glass pitchers of schmaltz (rendered chicken fat). We settled in and ordered drinks, while looking over the enormous menu. Some of us needed translations and interpretations of the Eastern European dishes. However, when the shirt-sleeved waiter came, Jerry ordered platters of food for everyone: hanger steak, brisket, roasted chicken, stuffed cabbage, derma, chopped liver with gribenes (tiny toasted flakes of chicken skin), roasted potatoes, and green beans with garlic. Jerry reminded everyone it was a Roumanian gastronome's delight.

It was a banquet for 10, although there were only seven at the table. Jerry's explanation was simple: "You can never have too much of a good thing." We whetted our palettes with Sammy's drink specialties: Vodka in frozen ice or Fox's U Bet chocolate egg creams for non-drinkers. Remarkably, we finished everything, including rice pudding for dessert. The meal was overwhelming but delicious.

If we had counted calories, we probably had consumed 3000 more than most of us were accustomed to eating.

"Well, fressers, what do you think?" Jerry said, referring to his diners with the Yiddish term for gluttons. "Is this serious cooking or what?"

Jerry paid the enormous check and had arranged for taxis to be waiting at Chrystie Street to take his guests home - a prime example of his largesse.

Charlie said afterward, "We need Jerry to remind us that we are not in a bubble on Madison Avenue."

Jerry continued as a valued friend and an important contributor to Charlie's and Jack's successful business. In an interesting romantic twist, his daughter married Jack Wayman's son Jack Jr. The wedding solidified business, social, and family ties that originated with a clever way to introduce Jerry Jordan: the Chicago limousine at the Consumer Electronics Show in 1975.

Saul Poliak, the Founder and President of Clapp & Poliak, a major producer of industrial trade shows

15

Saul Poliak and the Plant Engineering Show of 1967

S aul Poliak was an extraordinary trade show manager and an inspired and persevering innovator beyond all bounds as this story will attest. He was my first mentor in the trade show business.

His premier event, the National Plant Engineering & Maintenance Show was scheduled for January, 1967, at McCormick Place in Chicago. It was one of Clapp & Poliak's most successful shows and a major meeting place for manufacturing and the plant engineering industry. Exhibitors were confirmed and final payments received. Finished floor plans had been sent to Chicago contractors. Over 3,000 plant engineering and maintenance executives were registered, and more were expected onsite.

Saul shared this complete episode with me when I went to work for him a year later in 1968.

A week before the show opened, everything was set. Both exhibitors and attendees were primed for the event. Bulletins had been sent to exhibitors to remind them about shipping, set-up, travel, and hotels. Notices were delivered to attendees to remind them to make their arrangements for the following week. Everything was in place for a great trade show.

Then the unbelievable happened. McCormick Place was engulfed in flame and burned to the ground.

The scope of the fire was impossible to fathom. *Tribune* reporters and the photographer who raced to the scene sent word back to the Tribune Tower that McCormick Place was an inferno. The night editor was in shock. "It can't be," was his response.

The Chicago Tribune reported: "The night McCormick Place burned, the building that was supposed to be fireproof and outlast Rome's glories, was consumed frighteningly fast. Smoke was reported by janitors at 2:05 am on January 16th. By 2:30 am, when Fire Commissioner Robert Quinn arrived, he upgraded it to a five-alarm fire. Eighteen minutes later, he ordered the first special alarm. By 7 am, there was nothing but rubble."

McCormick Place burned to the ground with the blaze beginning at 2:05 am. It was nothing but rubble by 7 am that morning.

The huge Housewares Show scheduled to open that day was totally consumed by the fire. The roof of McCormick Place completely collapsed, and smoldering embers and water damage were all that remained of the hundred acres of what was once Chicago's finest convention center.

Trade show conventioneers for the Housewares Show were in hotel lobbies throughout the city were trying to understand what it all meant. Saul Poliak was trying to understand, too. His imminent Plant Engineering Show had just lost its venue.

Saul was, above all, a man of action. When he heard the shocking news at 7 am, he immediately got on the phone and called his longtime friend, Mert Thayer. Mert was the general manager of The International Amphitheatre in South Chicago, and Saul had him lock up the space for the following week.

Dozens of shows scrambled to find new homes. The National Sporting Goods Show moved to Navy Pier. The Chicago Auto Show moved to The International Amphitheater three weeks later. Saul did not have three weeks. He wanted his event to be as seamless as possible with the original McCormick Place schedule. Saul said he was lucky that Mert had the following week open at The Amp, as it was affectionately known in Chicago.

Owned by Armour and Company, The Amp was adjacent to Chicago's historic stock yards and had a long history. It was in Mayor Richard Daley's home precinct in South Chicago, known as Bridgeport. The Amp had cattle shows, rodeos, wrestling matches, and the National Republican Convention, where in 1952, Dwight D. Eisenhower was nominated for President. The NBA's Chicago Bulls played in The Amp for several years before they moved to their own arena. This would be the site of Saul's newly displaced show.

A month's work had to be accomplished in three days by Saul's managers. First on their checklist: the McCormick Place floor plan had to be redrawn for The Amp on South Halsted Street. Following that were 400 critical items that had to be carefully checked off, one by one. Each was essential in re-casting the event to the new facility. Exhibitors had to be contacted by phone and telegram. Service contractors were instructed to start over. They had to revise all their labor, warehousing, and freight orders. They had to confirm carpenters, expo workers, teamsters, and electricians for the new site. Registration services and convention bureaus altered their staff and schedules. Hotels honored or changed existing room reservations. Saul and his staff revamped their entire work/sleep/eat schedule.

Saul understood change and chaos. His first job was as a reporter in Mexico for *The Christian Science Monitor.*

In conversations with me, Saul explained, "There was never a time when we lost faith, but it was a daunting experience. There were challenges every hour. We literally did not sleep for 72 hours. In the end, we accomplished our goal of moving to The Amp, our new home in South Chicago. After an arduous week of non-stop crises, and advising each player of all the inalterable changes, we were ready for The Amp."

The Amp was ready for Saul. He and his managers arrived the first morning to supervise the set-up of the new show in the cold, drafty arena that would be their home for the next three days. A whole city of plant engineering exhibits was erected from the ground up in a space that had previously held live cattle shows with ambient smells still lingering on the bare concrete floor.

Mert Thayer was their host at the Amp. He was a rough and ready character and a wily landlord and for some, a rapscallion of the old school. He could have played Fagin corrupting orphans in Oliver Twist.

Mert was an opportunistic arena manager who booked every event that he could in his commodious, old building. He worked for the Armour owners, the Wood-Prince family, on a salary plus commission calculated on saving operating expense. His savings started with not providing heat in the winter or air conditioning in the summer. On frigid days in January, he went around in shirtsleeves, demonstrating his disdain for the cold. When show managers complained that The Amp was freezing, Mert merely shrugged his shoulders. "What are you talking about? It's comfortable for me," he'd say, extending his bare arms while union workers huddled by open fire pits to keep warm.

With great effort, the 1967 Plant Engineering Show installation was completed. Aisle carpeting was laid, registration counters set, signage hung, cleaning crews collected trash, exhibitors finished displays, and food concessionaires and coat check vendors made ready their counters for opening day.

On the day before the show opened, it started to snow. Unbeknownst to Saul, those first flakes were…the Chicago Blizzard of 1967. Over the course of 35 hours, 23 inches of snow blanketed the City of Chicago. It was a record snowfall reported by the U.S. Weather Service. Streets were clogged; cars, trucks, and buses were stranded on Michigan Avenue. All the major highways were at a standstill. Businesses were shuttered. Roofs collapsed. People died of exposure in poorly heated homes. The city was completely paralyzed.

Saul Poliak's Plant Engineering Show opened that day.

Saul and his three managers struggled to get to The Amp from The Palmer House Hotel downtown. They found a Red Line subway still operating that took them to a South Chicago train stop somewhat close to their destination. They then managed a ten-block walk in two feet of snow. Without cars on the road, walking on the street was the easiest way to get to the venue.

The Chicago Blizzard of 1967

Mert Thayer greeted them at the door. He'd slept in his office the night the snow started falling. He turned on the lights, unlocked the door, and like a shopkeeper of old, opened The Amp and was ready for business.

Slowly, others arrived. Exhibitors first. Then a few attendees. In the height of the blizzard, there were brave souls with warm coats and a work ethic. Saul and his managers were astounded. Their show, although crippled by the blizzard, managed to go on.

By the second day, more subways were running, and the traffic snarl had abated. A few more exhibitors and attendees managed the five miles from the Loop to South Chicago. It was not a normal show by any means, but it was a show, and show business was conducted.

Saul found solace in the 1967 event. "We met every challenge that nature and circumstance threw at us. Was the show successful – no. Did we succeed in keeping the show running – yes. Success is sometimes measured in relation to what would have happened if we had done nothing. The show certainly would have floundered. And as a result of our 1967 efforts, we continued with our 1968 show that flourished. Good sometimes comes out of bad."

To put 1967 in perspective, the Viet Nam war was raging in Southeast Asia. The Vietcong Tet offensive in Hue in February brought a destructive end to that citadel and the loss of thousands of American and Vietcong lives. Student riots were closing schools and universities throughout the United States.

Saul Poliak's greatest challenge, through fire and blizzard, required vision and perseverance, and his business survived. The Plant Engineering Show endured.

Tesla and Elon Musk are the darlings of the electric vehicle industry and Wall Street. This story is of an earlier time in the EV industry.

16

The Electric Vehicle Expo

Tesla is today's darling of the electric car industry and the New York Stock Exchange. Elon Musk, Tesla's founder, is a U.S. billionaire many times over and is the most successful electric vehicle producer in the world. In 2019, his firm rolled out 367,500 elegant EV models in facilities in the United States and China.

In 1977, Tesla did not exist, Elon Musk was not even born yet, and the fledging EV industry was just getting started. The Electric Auto Association (EEA), had formed in the 1970s to promote EV's to the American consumer. Their members were car wonks and start-up manufacturers, building cars in small facilities and family garages throughout the United States. Ford, GM, and Chrysler were also working on EVs, but they were experimental and not major production models. EV manufacturing was in its infancy.

Like Ethel Merman's song in *Gypsy*, small time EV developers had a dream.

Their dream was to build a battery-powered car that could operate a whole week without a recharge. Battery power, as Elon Musk learned 50 years later, was the key to successfully manufacturing electric vehicles in high volume for the automotive consumer.

Serious gas shortages in the 1970s had already wreaked havoc on the driving public with millions of cars waiting in lines for hours to fill up at gas stations. America needed a better solution. EAA also needed a better solution - to demonstrate EV practicality for the American public. A trade show could be the answer.

Charlie Snitow got a call from the executive director of EAA. The association wanted to talk about a new show that would demonstrate the viability of EV's for their industry.

At that time, Charlie and Bob Krakoff were co-presidents of Charlie's firm, and Bob was responsible for new shows. He had Reed Publishing's backing and wanted to generate business, just as Charlie had in former years.

Charlie and Bob conferred and agreed that electric vehicles were the 'next big thing.' Charlie's experience with the New York Auto Show and his long-time relationships with Ford, General Motors, Chrysler, and major car manufacturers, could be put to work as a natural progression toward EV technology. What neither of them knew was that most EAA members were not Ford, General Motors, or Chrysler. They were EV tinkerers, underfinanced, and without established production capability or knowhow.

Unaware of those shortcomings, Charlie and Bob agreed to produce the show. They appointed Jerry van Dyck, one of Charlie's managers, as the show director. His job would be to organize and sell EAA members and other EV producers to exhibit in their first-time event. The First Annual Electric Vehicle Expo & Conference was launched and scheduled for April, 1978, at the Baltimore Convention Center in Maryland.

Jerry had the distinction of starting the first annual SHOT Show for the gun industry which had grown into an enormous success. EV was a different industry with a different economy. He focused his efforts in earnest with sales calls to all EAA members. Those calls uncovered the quicksand that was the financial underpinning of the entire EV industry.

EAA's annual production in 1978 was only a Petri dish of cars. Less than 5,000 EVs were produced annually in 1977. Many were simply prototypes with electric motors and batteries under the hoods of existing Detroit models. They were similar to present day NASCAR racing cars, with hidden exotic engines under ordinary-looking production bodies.

By comparison, today's EV market has over 2 million vehicles produced annually. Ford, General Motors, Chrysler, and Toyota, are all in the hunt, and Tesla leads the way. China accounts for 60% of the total world EV production. The big breakthrough came with the advent of a robust lithium and cobalt battery, able to keep a car on the road for 200 miles without a recharge.

None of that battery technology was available in 1978. But Jerry was an intrepid salesman and sold 40 EV exhibitors into the new show. His exhibitors were mainly EAA members. Yet, altogether, they occupied only a fraction of the space available in the Baltimore Convention Center.

Charlie, with 25 years of experience in auto shows, took an active role to remedy the situation. He summoned his New York Auto Show contractors to fill the Baltimore exhibit hall with 10,000 yards of carpeting, stage lighting, and every accoutrement of a major auto show.

EV exhibitors enhanced Charlie's efforts with attractive models and presentations by EV technical experts. Live music, show glitz, and signage completed the upbeat carnival setting for the Baltimore crowd expected at the three-day show.

Bob Krakoff and Jerry were eager to build more show traffic and TV coverage for the event. They decided to stage a parade of their electric vehicles through the streets of Baltimore, concluding at the Convention Center. It would be like Barnum & Bailey circuses of old, when elephants led townsfolk to festive grounds and the opening of the big top tent. Parades created crowd excitement and generated attendance.

The Baltimore Sun and local TV affiliates were invited to cover this modern-day circus parade of cars. Nothing like it had ever been done before. Jerry was the parade marshal and established the route with the Baltimore Police Department and the city's Department of Transportation.

Anticipating a possible breakdown, Jerry had the foresight to hire two tow trucks to follow the event. Jerry's parade had 25 vehicles participating from his 40 exhibitors. He suspected a few Rube Goldberg EVs might not make it. He could not have anticipated the catastrophe that followed.

Of the 25 cars that started the parade, only 10 finished.

EVs were strewn throughout the entire 5-mile Baltimore parade route like disconnected dots. With engine hoods up, EV cars and their drivers were at a total standstill, stranded, waiting for a tow truck so they could be returned to the Convention Center.

Both tow trucks were busy all afternoon collecting cars and hauling them back to the show. *The Baltimore Sun* and local TV stations were compassionate, not saying much about the parade. They did report that battery life was a major limitation of EV production.

The show only lasted that one year. Charlie lamented, "We gave it a try. Sometimes cutting-edge shows are *too* ahead of their time. EVs in the show clearly had lousy technology under the hood. But if you don't try, you will never succeed. It was worthwhile to give this new technology a shot. Cutting edge is sometimes the bleeding edge as well."

Charlie Snitow's office had the latest phone system, but computers only stayed until the bill came.

17

Computers in a Time of No Computers

There were no computers in Charlie's office in the 1970s.

Betty Djerf changed all that. She was Charlie's administrative director for the Consumer Electronics Show. She was a forward-thinking manager and saw the need for computers to help Charlie run his business better.

She was clever, had a great sense of purpose and an upbeat personality. We often had a laugh together over coffee while sharing a Jack Wayman or CES story. Charlie was lucky to have a game player dedicated and willing to do any job in the office.

Mainframe computers were a standard in large organizations. Online systems were a necessity in banks, brokerage firms, insurance companies, and manufacturing organizations. It was the most efficient way to access the power of digital technology. Large companies accessed and expensed them on an hourly basis. Charlie's firm was a small office.

Starting from scratch with her online mainframe service, Betty taught herself Basic and set about to create an administrative system for Charlie's trade show operation. She spent hours after 5 o'clock with her online host. On most evenings, a new digital world awaited her. Betty learned programs, commands, and protocols to communicate with her new cyber friend.

She represented the entire Snitow organization in every aspect of her online experience, authorizing logins, pass codes, and expensing time. With great excitement, she would go to Charlie's office and show him printouts of her previous night's work.

"That's amazing, Betty," Charlie would say, "but I don't understand it. Why are you using the computer when most of it is already done by hand?" But like a doting father, Charlie would shrug and say, "I guess Betty knows what she's doing. Maybe it's good that she's bringing the computer age into the office."

There was only one problem. The hourly expense. The online programming expense was mounting every night with no one keeping track of it. Not even Betty.

The mainframe service invoice arrived quietly by mail. It had been two months since Betty had started her online programming.

"Holy smoke, Betty, $23,723.73 for two months of online service!" Charlie said. "What were you thinking?" As bright and forthcoming as any in his office, Betty had no answer.

In hindsight, $23,723.73 was just tuition for the educational foray into the awesome power of digital technology. IBM's desktops, Microsoft's Windows operating system, and the Internet were still in the future. Betty was ahead of her time. And being one of Charlie's favorites, the invoice was quietly paid without further comment. Charlie had a generous way of allowing honest mistakes even if they were expensive.

Betty's online adventure was a great whisper story in the office. She took to wearing prescription sunglasses for a while to avoid unwanted eye contact.

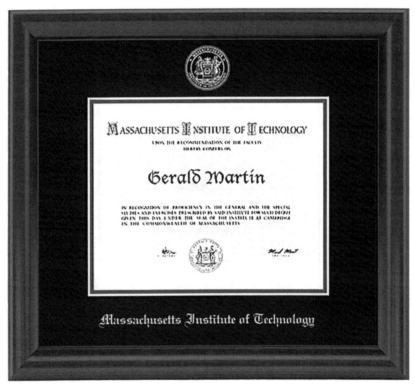

This story is about Dr. Martin's PhD diploma.

18

Dr. Martin's Diploma

Charlie Snitow's most talented sales manager was Jerry Martin, a former Marine who never finished high school. He was a major income producer of the multi-million-dollar New York Automobile Show. Thanks to Jerry's dedication, he and Charlie developed the show into the hallmark industry event it became. Recognizing and holding onto talent was Charlie's strength, and he made sure Jerry was well compensated for his efforts. They enjoyed a dynamic mentoring relationship.

Jerry was a voracious reader and a sponge for information. He made it his business to know everything about Ford, General Motors, Chrysler, and every other domestic and international car maker. His knowledge was mainly memorized *Automotive News* clippings, but impressive all the same. He could spew Detroit-talk for hours on styling, fuel injection, and emission standards.

Forever inspired to add new trade shows to his portfolio, in 1972, Charlie launched the International Building Show. It focused on the fabrication of new homes and commercial buildings, and Buckminster Fuller, the legendary designer of the geodesic dome, was the featured speaker. Exhibits would include innovations in wind, thermal, and solar energy. Since Jerry had free time from the Auto Show, he agreed to be the sales manager of that section of the event. His prospects were high-tech energy companies, many funded by universities and scientific institutions.

Jerry was known as a master of flattery and great storytelling. Like Victor Borge, he could imitate any dialect. One of Jerry's great sales talents was assuming the persona of the prospect he was trying to sell.

With energy people, he became an expert on BTU's, Icelandic thermals, and wind velocity. With CEOs who were university PhDs, Jerry also became a PhD. He simply matched their title.

"Hi, Dr. Martin here," he'd say, introducing himself. "I read about your new program in *Scientific American*. We have a new marketplace for your thermal energy system that is the only energy show in the United States this year."

However, Dr. Martin was often reminded of how elitist his learned colleagues were.

"Was just on the phone with a top PhD from Harvard," Jerry lamented. "Just once, I'd like to talk to a guy who didn't remind me that he was a PhD. What a bunch of fakers these guys are."

In talking with Charlie one afternoon, I off-handedly suggested, "Why don't we make Jerry a real PhD?"

Charlie smiled and said, "If you're so smart, go to it."

Passing by a stationery store the next day, I saw sample diplomas in the window. All that was needed was Jerry's name, a PhD designation from a leading university, a gold wafer, and a glass frame. I bought everything and brought it to Charlie's office to assemble.

"Charlie, you've got to sign this to make it official," I said.

The diploma read: *Gerald Martin, PhD, Thermal Sciences, Massachusetts Institute of Technology; Charles Snitow, President.* This would be a classic joke on Dr. Martin.

"We have a surprise for you, Jerry," I said, leaning on Jerry's door jam. "Come to Charlie's office."

Charlie had the framed diploma on his desk and staff members were gathered behind him. With great dignity, Charlie said, "There is a special occasion that comes only once in a person's life. It is with great solemnity that we confer on Gerald Martin (that's you, bubeleh), the title of PhD, Thermal Sciences, Massachusetts Institute of Technology."

Some of the group stifled smiles. We all looked to see Jerry's reaction.

To our surprise, Jerry did not react as expected. His doctorate was not a joke. Almost teary, Jerry simply looked at the framed certificate. It confirmed something he knew about himself. He deserved it. While just a stationary-store-bought diploma with Charlie's signature, it had special significance. His mentor and benefactor had conferred it. We understood the PhD was long overdue.

He hung his framed diploma proudly in his office, the same way Charlie hung his Cornell College and Law School degrees. The joke was on us. It was the Scarecrow's diploma bestowed to him by the Wizard in *The Wizard of Oz*.

From that day on, Jerry was Dr. Martin, PhD.

McCormick Place employees have their own patois and code of conduct.

19

I Get My Information on the Bottom Rung

Bernie went by his first name, but everyone knew him.

Bernie was the daytime guard service supervisor during the National Hardware Show in McCormick Place in 1978. Being on the same radio network frequency as his guard service, we became well aware of Bernie. During his 8-hour shift, we'd hear his messages to his crew and to our management staff. The man was memorable.

Like most workmen at McCormick, Bernie knew his place in the building's hierarchy, was hard working, and never complained. He was in constant contact with the guards on his shift who were stationed at the entrances and perimeter of the show. They were responsible for checking show badges, crowd control, and maintaining a fire watch. They were essential. The original McCormick Place had burned down in 1967, and for years after, the Chicago Fire Department had a fully-equipped fire truck parked inside McCormick with a full crew to prevent fires from ever occurring again.

McCormick Place, and the trade shows that leased space there, depended on tradesmen like Bernie to pull the show together. Teamsters, carpenters, decorators, electricians, guard services, and building employees, totaled more than 800 at work on the National Hardware Show. These crews had their own patois. Chicago, to them, was just two syllables: Shka-go.

They not only had their own jargon, but were also able craftsmen who could assemble a complex exhibit from scratch. Often, they did so without printed instructions and had it connected to electrical power – and fully operational – within a three or four-hour period. These crews literally built cities of exhibits on bare hall floors in a single day or two of set up in order to have them ready for attendees on opening day. They were well paid, took great pride in their work, and were the backbone of the trade show business in Chicago. If a show succeeded under their watch, they knew it would be back.

On the other hand, Bernie's guards were less experienced than most of the tradesmen and were often new hires fresh off the street. They needed constant shepherding to stay at their posts. Bernie used his radio and rode his motor scooter to each guard post to corral guards and keep them in line.

Bernie was constantly on the radio, and we in show management were the impromptu on-air audience for his unique language.

"I get my information on the bottom rung." His recognized importance.

"I'm not the first and not the last to know." His path of scuttlebutt.

"You dare 'cent do it." His cautionary warning.

"I told him, and he's told." His no-nonsense method of correcting his guards.

"You can't never be too early or too late." His reminder to staff about timeliness.

"You count your chickens when you come to them." His problem-solving approach.

"Don't ask me about what I don't know." His acknowledged lack of information.

"Wisdom never comes easy." His experience with young guards.

The National Hardware Show was a 3-day event, with an additional day to set up and a day to move out. Bernie was a kind of Yogi Berra during those five days, yet completely unaware of the uniqueness of his language.

Charlie offered a commentary: "Bernie was not an entertainer. He was a hard-working guard supervisor who did his job. He was an original, that's for sure. But we loved him for his special gifts."

Charlie Snitow's charming carriage house offices at Sniffin Court

20

Sniffin Court

Reed Publishing of Boston bought Charlie's trade show company in 1968. Seven years later, Reed brought in an executive, Bob Krakoff, to work with Charlie to manage the business. Like Reed's president, Saul Goldweitz, and chairman, Norman Cahners, Bob was an alumnus of the eminent Harvard Business School.

The HBS approach to managing and growing a business signaled changes and challenges for Charlie and his trade show enterprise. New trade shows were added and outside people brought in to run them. Krakoff initiated weekly sales reports from the sales managers for each show. He needed the sales information for his own weekly dispatches to Boston. The business style which was classic Charlie, on the other hand, was less by the book and more easy-going. He loved trade shows and the roustabout characters who were still a part of it. He made a lot of money for his company and himself, but it was instinctive. Charlie did not need weekly sales reports to know how a show was doing. He could tell by overhearing his sales managers on the phone. He knew when sales were lagging and how to bring them to profitability. But Krakoff was now in charge and 'times were a-changin', as Bob Dylan's song reminded.

It was no surprise when Krakoff suggested Charlie might be happier relocating to an office of his own. Charlie expected this and started his search in earnest.

"We saw a lot of offices around Grand Central. Law offices, medical offices, advertising offices. None spoke to me as a happy place to work.

"One day we saw a carriage house on East 36th Street. It was in a lovely muse known as Sniffin Court, a forgotten cobblestoned cul-de-sac with eight stables built for horse-drawn carriages. Charming carriage houses were totally redone as pied-a-terres for some lucky New Yorkers - like me.

"The Sniffin Court space was available, and Krakoff and Reed were only too happy to get rid of me. It was a perfect setting for a new chapter in my life, and it was inevitable."

The building had a charming Dutch door, a high-ceilinged living room, a small kitchen in the basement, and a small bedroom for anyone missing a train from too much merriment. Charlie stocked his cellar with wine, French Champagne, and plenty of Polish vodka. He made sure he had his Cuban cigars. One wag suggested that with cigars, champagne, and vodka, Sniffin Court should have been called 'Sniff and Snort.'

Not only did this location house Charlie's working headquarters, but it also became a grand salon for friends and admirers. It was Dorothy Parker's Roundtable at the Algonquin. With Charlie presiding, there was a coterie of amateur cooks and invited pals and business guests for lunch almost every day. Some came to say hello, others to seek advice, others to offer tempting investment or business opportunities.

One Broadway producer wanted Charlie to be an angel investor in August Wilson's new play, *Ma Rainey's Black Bottom*. An art dealer offered a James McNeill Whistler watercolor of the London wharf. A stage director wanted Charlie to co-produce Noel Coward's, *Blithe Spirit* as a musical. All these opportunities were welcomed enthusiastically, some taken advantage of with gusto. Sniffin Court was an ideal place to consider these fascinating proposals while finishing coffee and crème brûlée.

Being the lawyer that he was, Charlie challenged his luncheon guests for their opinions. "What do you think? Should I invest in *Ma Rainey's Black Bottom*? I spent years investing in trade shows, but maybe I should have been a Broadway producer. I would have lost my shirt, but I would have had a hellava good time," he said.

Occasionally, Charlie would invite his former Reed colleagues over for drinks. He welcomed Krakoff and the young Turks running his business. He was hospitable and made sure his guests had drinks, cigars, and bon amie. He was especially solicitous of newcomers. "I may need a job someday, and I don't want to burn any bridges," Charlie quipped.

Bob Krakoff continued as the president of Charlie's former company, adding shows and expanding the business. Bob was capable, but the special charm Charlie cultivated in his business was not Krakoff's style. Bob's shows had the proper Harvard Business School profit and loss quotient, but little reliance on vodka, Champagne, and Cuban cigars.

Charlie was sanguine about change. "There is an old Arabic proverb, 'The dogs bark, but the caravan moves on.' I am happy with my second life at Sniffin Court. I wish the best for Reed and their business."

It's a high-level challenge to find excellent speakers for the HPC AI on Wall Street.

21

The Challenge of Landing an Industry Star

As a trade show producer for over 30 years, my profession provided a wealth of experience and contacts with innovators of the highest order. At most of my events, I organized the conference as well as the exhibits and show. It was my task to find outstanding speakers as a draw for an audience of industry professionals. Important people mattered. The more esteemed and newsworthy, the better the turnout.

Here is an example: at the September 2010 HPC (High Performance Computing) for Wall Street, I was looking for a recognized industry leader as my keynote speaker from a major technology firm. The perfect person would be a high-level executive who would also bring their firm onboard as a major sponsor. Keeping abreast of current events on Wall Street had become a necessity, and my morning reads included *The New York Times, The Wall Street Journal, The Financial Times*, and the *New York Post*, to keep up with technology, become familiar with new buzz words, and to find potential speakers. An article in *The Wall Street Journal* piqued my interest. I read about a legendary electronics engineer and entrepreneur who had co-founded Sun Microsystems and had recently founded and launched Arista Networks in 2008. His new firm was creating ultra-high-speed networks and switches for a new echelon of Wall Street traders.

Michael Lewis, the well-known Wall Street journalist and cyber-guru, wrote about these high-frequency traders in his book, *Flash Boys,* and described their transactions at one-hundred-millionth of a second on fiber-optic networks. Wall Street traders were transacting instant trades from New York to Chicago, Denver, and London, at the speed of light.

Andy Bechtolsheim, Arista Network's CEO, was mentioned in the article as responsible for developing these cutting-edge switches with nanosecond latency. Born in Germany, he had been a student at the Technical University of Munich where he'd garnered a physics prize, but bored with his studies, he'd won a Fulbright to Carnegie Mellon University where he obtained his master's degree. In 1977, he transferred to Stanford University and became a PhD student in electrical engineering.

Another interesting distinction written about, was how Andy had provided early funding for Sergey Brin and Larry Page. In 1988, after meeting with them and discussing the search engine they were designing, he wrote them a check for $100,000. That was before the two even incorporated their company - Google - and his sagacious investment became worth almost $7 billion.

I wanted Andy for my opening keynote speaker, and I wanted Arista to become a Gold Sponsor, joining IBM, Intel, Hewlett Packard, and Cisco, as well as other Silicon Valley and digital industry giants already slated to speak. The day after I read that article, I was on the phone to his administrative assistant in Santa Clara, California.

"Good morning. I'm Russ Flagg, the conference director of the HPC on Wall Street, and I wanted to check Mr. Bechtolsheim's schedule to see if he would be available to speak at our conference, September 13th, Monday, in New York. We want him as our keynote speaker this year.

"The 10th annual conference is for Wall Street managing directors and technology VPs. The recent article in *The Wall Street Journal* is amazing and really covers what a great company Mr. Bechtolsheim has launched with Arista Networks."

His assistant was polite but short and direct. "Mr. Bechtolsheim is an extremely busy man. I'm sure he will not be able to commit to any speaking engagements any time soon."

I replied, "We certainly understand. We want to wish Arista and Mr. Bechtolsheim great success, and on the off chance that he *is* free in September, we will be sending him an invitation to speak. We also want your marketing people to know about sponsorship for our show. We already have IBM, Intel, HP, and Cisco on board, and we would like Arista to join us as well."

"Thanks for thinking of us, Mr. Flagg, but I can't hold out any hope for his speaking," she replied firmly. She did suggest we contact the Arista marketing department, and she gave me a name.

This was the inflection point in my search for a keynote speaker, and in a broader sense, the challenge of our trade show business. I could have easily accepted her polite refusal and moved on, hearing the perfect excuse for not having an Arista speaker. Or I could accept a more daunting challenge and convince both Mr. Bechtolsheim and his assistant to agree to attend the conference and have an outstanding speaker for my efforts.

Selecting speakers for my conferences was a hit or miss proposition. There were always mediocre speakers available - industry executives that wanted to flog their wares and provide a self-serving product pitch. There were others - technocrats with a blizzard of hard-to-read computer slides to challenge any audience's patience and attention. To find the right balance required some research, surveys, and luck. Who do past attendees and leading authorities recommend? The challenge was to find *new* speakers who were recognized authorities in their business. That was my goal with Andy Bechtolsheim. He was new, had not spoken at many conferences, and the Wall Street Journal article was a compelling endorsement for him and his new venture.

What would Charlie have said when faced with the challenge of a strong 'no'? My guess was that he would have reminded me: "Real selling begins when someone says 'no.' It compels you to overcome reasonable and legitimate objections. That's what our business is all about. Convincing people to do what is in their best interests (and ours)."

My next phone call was propitious – because the new Arista marketing contact was positive, upbeat, and eager to put Arista in the limelight. She was the polar opposite of Andy's door-keeper and protector. Luck was on my side in my campaign to get Andy Bechtolsheim to speak.

However, after countless phone calls, emails, and written proposals to my contact and others at Arista over a five-month period...nothing.

Finally, I received an unexpected phone call from my marketing friend at Arista in August, 30 days before the conference.

"Russell, if, and it is a big if, Andy Bertolsheim can make it to New York on September 13th, what do you want him to talk about?" she asked cautiously.

After catching my breath, I recovered, and answered, "Well, Andy knows more about high-speed networks and switches than anyone. I suggest he provide a state-of-the-art talk on high frequency trading and what Arista is building for Flash Boys, the guys Michael Lewis wrote about in his book."

Putting the onus back on me, she said, "Okay Russell, put it in writing. I want a formal proposal, and I'll circulate it around to see what the bosses think." And good as her word, within a week, I received confirmation that I could promote Andy as an 'invited' keynoter, subject to his final travel schedule and arrangement of client meetings in New York with Wall Street customers. I had success after five months.

The rest of Andy's planning over the next 30 days was in the hands of his capable (and now), extremely friendly administrative assistant. I received his bio and photo and the title of his keynote from her. We worked together to take care of his hotel stay at the Roosevelt and adjusted our program to accommodate his New York meeting schedule. Thanks to my Arista marketing friend, Arista Networks also agreed to join us as a Gold Sponsor with an exhibit booth featuring their ultra-high-speed network systems and switches.

Meeting Andy for the first time on Monday morning, preceding his keynote, was a special treat. He was tall, low-key, and courtly. Appropriately attired, he wore his Silicon Valley uniform: an elegant blue blazer and designer jeans, with an open-collar, white shirt. Andy had a confident, easy going charm, and it brought me tremendous pleasure to introduce him to the assembled audience of 300 Wall Street technology executives in the classic, spacious Roosevelt Hotel Grand Ballroom.

In addition to delivering a successful and highly informative talk, Andy managed his schedule so he could attend some of the other Grand Ballroom conference sessions that morning. I heard feedback from other speakers and attendees stating that his presence was felt; he proved to be a good listener as well as a good speaker. Both he and Arista were the stars of the exhibit hall with their cutting-edge technology for high-speed transactions, networking, and data storage, employing their latest Gigabit Ethernet systems.

My HPC on Wall Street event continued annually in September at the Roosevelt Hotel, and Arista Networks became an important sponsor in succeeding shows. Three years later, I welcomed Jayshree Ulla, Arista Networks' new CEO, as a keynote speaker for the program. Jayshree, like Andy, was a successful Silicon Valley engineer, a seasoned corporate executive, and a billionaire.

Equally engaging, Jayshree Ulla was an elegant person that I had the pleasure of meeting and introducing at her conference session. Arista Networks was an innovator in cloud networking and her program highlighted her company's role in the development of the cloud. It was a great success, dovetailing with Wall Street's insatiable thirst for the latest information on speed, low latency, and cloud data storage. Jayshree was a brilliant speaker and advanced Arista Networks as a major American computer networking force with an annual revenue of $2.4 billion.

Meeting, as well as being inspired by, successful billionaires was a by-product of being in a position to offer a speaking platform to the most important and talented people in various industries. Inviting newsworthy industry leaders to a forum that could advance new technology and innovation for Wall Street or other markets has made for a stimulating career. I'm proud to say that the HPC AI on Wall Street holds its place as an essential Wall Street forum to this day.

Trade shows, both virtual and in-person, have taken on a life of their own, with intrepid entrepreneurs leading the way.

22

What's Next?

Covid-19's relentless attack on the trade show industry brought originally scheduled 2020 events to a grinding halt. Approximately 97% of them were cancelled, as reported by The Center for Exhibition Industry Research (CEIR), headquartered in Dallas, Texas.

"The devastation of the trade show, exposition, and in-person event industry does not need another recap or reminder of where we are or how we got there," states CEIR in their recent, 'What's Next for the Exposition and Trade Show Business in 2021?'

An Oxford Economics/CEIR study previously reported that over 13,000 trade shows are held annually in the United States, 45% of the world total of 27,000 events. CEIR estimates the annual dollar volume of U.S. events held in 2019 exceeded $100 million. (My own opinion is that the 2020 trade show economic loss in the U.S. will be billions of dollars.)

CEIR is not alone in their 2020 findings of losses. *The New York Times* reported that the United States is estimated to have sustained $16 trillion in economic losses due to Covid-19. As of this writing, it has been 13 months since Covid-19 was first identified in Wuhan, China in December, 2019. Our trade show business has since been transformed.

Flagg Management Inc., in partnership with Tabor Communications Inc., has produced a high-performance computing and artificial intelligence trade show (HPC AI), for the last three years. We were successful in producing the 2018 and 2019 HPC AI for Wall Street in New York at the Roosevelt Hotel, with an excellent response from attendees and financial services vendors.

In 2020 we produced the HPC AI for Wall Street as a virtual event, in casualty response to Covid-19. It required a new and sophisticated level of broadcasting: sponsors and exhibitors featured their own web pages and home page branding and logos, speakers gave live presentations through Zoom from home offices. The show was successful in holding a place in its annual September timeframe, as it had for the past 20 years. It was much more expensive to put on than the previous year's live trade show at the Roosevelt. (That historic, 1,200-room Grand Central hotel on Madison Avenue, sadly, was a fatality of Covid-19. It has closed for good, as a result of a year's lost revenue from business travelers and commercial meetings and shows.)

Like the Roosevelt, many live-event colleagues are gone. The number of trade show professionals out of work as a result of Covid-19 is appalling and a national loss of immense talent. My hope is that they will return when America's population receives Covid-19 immunization in greater numbers to establish a true herd protection. This is essential for live events to recommence.

Two events occurred in January, 2021, that reflect on the vitality of the trade show business in the American economy. Sheldon Adelson, the founder of Comdex, the original 1980's blockbuster Computer Retailer Show, died at 87 on January 11th. He'd started life in Dorchester, a rough and tumble Boston neighborhood, and found his calling in trade shows. Shelley used his acumen in shows to build hotels, casinos, newspapers, and a prospering business that extended from the United States to Israel. By the end of his life, he'd amassed a $40 billion empire, including casino/hotels in Las Vegas; Macau; Singapore; and Bethlehem, PA.

On the Monday he died, CES 2021 (the Consumer Electronics Show), opened as a virtual four-day event with almost 2,000 exhibitors, major industry sponsors, and speakers from the CEO ranks of electronic corporations around the globe. CES in 2020, by contrast, was live and the largest electronics trade show in the world with over 170,000 attendees flying into Las Vegas to occupy every hotel to attend their industry's annual mega event with thousands of exhibitors as diverse as Microsoft with their cloud storage systems and Ford Motor Company with their computerized driverless cars. These two events are bookends of the industry that I am a part of, and may serve as a preview of what lies ahead.

Whether in-person or virtual, dedicated players in the trade show business have always thrived on two qualities: optimism, exemplified by Charlie Snitow, and determination, exhibited in Saul Poliak. We need a balance of both for our industry to prosper. I am confident new players will emerge with the chutzpah to carry on the vital, creative, and lucrative trade show industry.

About the Author

Russ celebrates his 85th birthday with too many candles.

Russell Flagg is the president of Flagg Management Inc., a New York corporation, dedicated to the management of trade shows throughout the United States.

Russ started with Alcoa, in Pittsburgh, Pennsylvania, working in advertising and marketing, selling aluminum products to American businesses. He then moved to Remington International, in Bridgeport, Connecticut, as an export manager, marketing to international electronics dealers in Europe and the Middle East.

Clapp & Poliak came next, learning the trade show business with a small, but important, industrial event firm. Saul Poliak was his mentor and friend.

Working for Charlie Snitow, the legendary producer of dealer and consumer shows, was next on Russ Flagg's career path. Charlie, too, became a mentor and valued friend in the business.

Experiences with Saul Poliak and Charlie Snitow left an indelible impression. Working alongside these intrepid innovators, Russ gained the confidence and know-how to launch his own company, Flagg Management, Inc. For over 30 years, his company has produced new shows in accounting, human resources, sales and marketing, fixed income, and Wall Street technology.

Russ lives in New York with his artist and graphic designer wife Holley Flagg. He graduated from Syracuse University, served in the Army in Korea as a company commander, and enjoys photography as a creative outlet.

Flagg Management, Inc. Shows Over the Last 30 Years

New York Accounting Show

California Accounting Show

Midwest Accounting Show

New Jersey Accounting Show

HPC/AI for Wall Street (High Performance Computing/Artificial Intelligence)

SEF-CON, (Investment Derivatives Conference and Show)

Fixed Income Conference

Human Resources Conference and Show

Disaster Recovery Conference and Show

Automotive Marketing Services Show

Tax Advantage Investment Conference

Sales and Marketing Show

Plant Engineering Show

Great American Firehouse Show

French Fashion Show

The New York Cash Exchange

FIM-New York (Financial Investment Management)

FIM-West (Financial Investment Management)

FIM-Chicago (Financial Investment Management)

Made in the USA
Middletown, DE
31 July 2021